Every Day with Jesus

SEP/OCT 2018

Ten Words

'Only be careful, and watch yourselves closely so that
you do not forget... or let them fade from your heart
as long as you live.' Deuteronomy 4:9

Selwyn Hughes

Revised and updated by Mick Brooks

© CWR 2018. Dated text previously published as *Every Day with Jesus:
The Sinai Revelation* (July/August 1990) by CWR.
This edition revised and updated for 2018 by Mick Brooks.

CWR, Waverley Abbey House, Waverley Lane, Farnham, Surrey GU9 8EP, UK **Tel: 01252 784700**
Email: mail@cwr.org.uk Registered Charity No. 294387. Registered Limited Company No. 1990308.

Where possible, every effort has been made to ensure that these devotional notes contain the correct permissions and
references. Please contact the Publisher directly for any further permissions information.

Cover image: Adobestock
Quiet Time image: Pixabay/joergweitz
Printed in England by Linney

MIX
Paper from
responsible sources
FSC® C015900

CWR

A word of introduction...

It is said that there are two types of people in the world: those who like lists, and those who don't. In many ways, the Ten Words that Selwyn explores in this issue could be described as God's top ten list. Although this is probably among one of the most misunderstood lists ever compiled, never have such a few words shaped so much. These are the words that form the foundations of a number of legal systems and government structures, which people of all faiths and none recognise as fundamental to civilisation and community living. They are not primarily a list of do's and don'ts thrown down by an angry, unpredictable and petulant god. God is a God of love: He is not just loving, He *is* Love. Love's very nature is other-centred, looking to give, serve and nurture; to bring about the highest good in another and to share life.

These Ten Words of God are given to enable us to grow and develop in our relationship with Him, and then with one another. When people would sometimes ask Selwyn what he considered to be the priorities of the Christian life, he would frequently reply: 'Loving involvement with God, and loving involvement with others.' Selwyn's life message, I suppose, was that we first grow in our relationship with God and then learn to live life well with others – and that would have been his heart and prayer for you when he first penned this issue.

Mick Brooks, Consulting Editor

 Free small group resource to accompany this issue can be found at **www.cwr.org.uk/extra**

The *EDWJ* Facebook community is growing!
To join the conversation visit **www.facebook.com/edwjpage**

God's blueprint for living

FOR READING & MEDITATION – EXODUS 20:1–21

'Do not be afraid. God has come... so that the fear of God will be with you to keep you from sinning.' (v20)

We begin today an in-depth exploration of the Ten Commandments – the divine blueprint for living, given several thousand years ago by God to Moses on the barren summit of a majestic peak in the Sinai peninsular. It seems to me that with the widespread ethical confusion going on all around us, we need to take a new look at these old principles and get it into our hearts and minds that they are more than just ancient documents with a fascinating historical interest. They are as relevant today as the day on which they were first given.

Research conducted with over 20,000 churchgoers in a city in the United States found that only one in 100 could recall the Ten Commandments, and only 15 in 100 could name the book of the Bible in which they are recorded. The Ten Commandments were one of the first things I was taught to memorise as a child, and although they did not give me a complete picture of God (that came later when I came to know Jesus and began to understand the truths of the New Testament), they nevertheless generated within me a sincere respect for God and His people.

Many people – even some Christians – consider the Ten Commandments to be as hard and as cold as the tablets of stone on which they were written, and they cannot imagine them to be the steps that lead to a fulfilled and satisfied existence. A man once said to me: 'Keeping to the Ten Commandments gives people a jaundiced view of life.' Please let me assure you that when properly understood, the Ten Commandments show us the way, not to a jaundiced living but to a joyous living. And over the next eight weeks, my prayer is for us to discover this to be true.

FURTHER STUDY

Deut. 10:1–13;
Josh. 24:11–15;
Eccl. 12:13

1. What did the Lord ask of Israel?

2. What choice did Joshua give to Israel?

Gracious and loving Father, help me as I begin this quest for light and illumination on something that at first seems cold and forbidding. Enable me to see that not only do You set high standards – You also supply the strength to attain them. Amen.

'Ten Words'

FOR READING & MEDITATION – DEUTERONOMY 4:1–14

'Only be careful, and watch yourselves closely so that you do not forget... or let them slip from your heart' (v9)

Today we ask ourselves: what exactly are the Ten Commandments? You might agree with the person who described them as 'God's law for a lawless world – the principles and precepts by which the soul of man must be eternally judged.' Some commentators claim that some of the Commandments overlap, and maintain that they should not be seen as ten distinct commands. However, Exodus 34:28 clearly says, 'And he wrote on the tablets the words of the covenant – the Ten Commandments.' In the Hebrew, the expression 'the Ten Commandments' is literally 'the Ten Words' – 'Word' in this context meaning a royal edict, the mandate of a king. Hence, with reference to God it means a royal, authoritative proclamation, a divine mandate that cannot be denied. The Greek word for the Ten Commandments is *Decalogue*, and this again reflects the idea of 'Ten Words'.

FURTHER STUDY

Deut. 6;
Jer. 3:21;
Isa. 51:11–16

1. What did the children of Israel have to be careful about?

2. What were they prone to?

To me, one of the greatest messages of the Ten Commandments is just that: they are much more than a code of ethics (they need a context, and that context is God Himself). We simply cannot separate morality (ethics) from God – the very creator and anchor of life itself. It is alarming that the era in which we live in the Western world is one where there are no moral absolutes, with many saying God and ethics should be seen as two separate issues. As the book of Judges highlights (see Judg. 21:25), when everyone follows their own set of moral values without any reference to God it is, in my opinion, the beginning of the end of a civilised and smooth-running society. We need to learn to understand these Ten Words so as not to fail our own and future generations.

God our Father, help us to hold fast to that which You have given, so that, as those who came before us have passed on a strong deposit to us, we may pass on a strong deposit to others. In Jesus' name we pray. Amen.

Not merely ethics

FOR READING & MEDITATION – ROMANS 3:19–31

'This righteousness from God comes through faith in Jesus Christ to all who believe.' (v22)

We continue with the thought we touched on yesterday – that one of the greatest messages of the Ten Commandments is that you cannot separate ethics from God. The very structure of the Commandments challenges this thought. Of the Ten Words of Sinai, the first four deal with mankind's relationship to God and the remaining six with man's relationship to mankind.

Interestingly, in so many discussions on the Ten Commandments, the first four are often passed over and the emphasis falls on the last six. But this is unfaithful to the Decalogue – it's only half the truth. Why do people do this? Well, perhaps it is because in order to live well (in a biblical sense), one needs to be in a relationship with God. Those with no faith, therefore, perhaps skip over the first four Commandments because it makes them feel uncomfortable to be faced with the challenge of giving their lives to the living God. And we all tend to avoid the things that make us feel uncomfortable.

As you work your way with me through these meditations on the Ten Words, keep this thought before you: the Ten Commandments are not simply a statement on ethics, but are the terms of the covenant between God and humanity. We will never fully grasp the deep meaning underlying the Ten Commandments until we see that they are to be lived out in the context of a relationship with God. We are all created to live in a right relationship with God and those around us. When God gave these Ten Words, they were more than just a set of rules to live by. Each one carries with it a principle for living that enhances our everyday experience.

FURTHER STUDY

Psa. 119:129–138; 48:1–11; 97:2

1. What is the foundation of God's throne?

2. What was the psalmist's testimony?

My Father and my God, deepen my understanding of the truth that the closer my relationship with You, the more I discover of You. In Jesus' name. Amen.

Never out of date

FOR READING & MEDITATION – PSALM 119:137–142

'Your righteousness is everlasting and your law is true.' (v142)

Christians hold a surprising number of different views and attitudes on these Ten Words. Some might say that they were relevant for the time in which they were given, but in today's culture, we need a different set of moral principles and guidelines. Others might say: 'The Ten Commandments are not particularly useful for Christians because we are not under law, but under grace.' And there are some Christians who say: 'Once we are saved by grace we are free from all moral obligations and principles; we can then live as we choose.' I once heard about a church leader addressing a school assembly like this: 'The Ten Commandments should be treated like a school examination paper – "six only to be attempted"' – the implication being that as long as you make an effort to obey some, then it won't matter too much if you don't attempt them all.

FURTHER STUDY

Psa. 19:1–11;
Rom. 7:12–14;
1 Tim. 1:8

1. How did the psalmist sum up the law?

2. How did Paul describe the law?

The question, then, to come to grips with before we go any further is this: are the Ten Commandments obsolete – or absolute? Are they as true for today as they were for the day on which they were first given to Moses on Mount Sinai? As I have said, it is my belief that they are God's original framework for life and living, which does not change from one generation to another. Knowledge is increasing at such a rate that titles of some subjects have to be replaced every few years. Some books written ten years ago are now out of date. But that is not how it is with the Ten Commandments. God's Words are never out of date. They apply with as much authority to the men and women of the twenty-first century as they did to the men and women of past centuries.

Father, help me to live in the good of Your divine framework and impress even more deeply into my spirit a deep understanding that the Ten Words You spoke at Sinai are not only unchanged, but unchanging. Amen.

CWR Ministry Events

PLEASE PRAY FOR THE TEAM

DATE	EVENT	PLACE	PRESENTER(S)
6 Sep	Improving Your Pastoral Care	Waverley Abbey House	Andy Peck
14–16 Sep	Inspiring Women Autumn Weekend: God's Abundance	WAH	Rosie Morgan and Lynn Penson
21–23 Sep	Bible Discovery Weekend	WAH	Philip Greenslade
27 Sep	Experiencing God	WAH	Andy Peck
27 Sep	The Bible in an Evening	WAH	Andy Peck
4 Oct	Reaching the Next Generation	WAH	Andy Peck and Martin Saunders
6 Oct	The Unexpected Journey	WAH	Rachel Wright
9 Oct	Inspiring Women Autumn Day: Women of Courage	WAH	Anne Calver and Clare Lambert
10 Oct	Honesty Over Silence	WAH	Patrick Regan
11 Oct	Work, Rest and Play	WAH	Andy Peck
17 Oct	The Centre Brain	WAH	Steve Adams
18 Oct	Praying like your Life Depends on it	WAH	Andy Peck
19 Oct	Insight into Shame	WAH	Heather Churchill
30 Oct	Inspiring Women Autumn Evening	WAH	Judy Moore

Please pray for our students and tutors on our ongoing BA Counselling programme at Waverley Abbey College (which takes place at Waverley Abbey House), as well as our Certificate in Christian Counselling and MA Counselling qualifications.

We would also appreciate prayer for our ongoing ministry in Singapore and Cambodia, as well as the many regional events that will be happening around the UK this year.

For further information and a full list of CWR's courses, seminars and events, call **(+44) 01252 784719** or visit **www.cwr.org.uk/courses**

You can also download our free Prayer Track, which includes daily prayers, from **www.cwr.org.uk/prayertrack**

The timing of the Commandments

FOR READING & MEDITATION – GALATIANS 5:16–26

'Since we live by the Spirit, let us keep in step with the Spirit.' (v25)

Before we examine in detail each of the Ten Commandments, we ask ourselves: why were the Ten Words given to the children of Israel after they had left Egypt rather than before? I think one reason is because God wanted to emphasise that redemption comes first and how to live comes second. The Exodus comes before the Commandments. Salvation leads, lifestyle follows. If the 'how to live' came before salvation, we would be in danger of thinking salvation is by works. And to mix salvation with works is the Galatian heresy of mixing law and grace.

FURTHER STUDY

Rom. 6;
Psa. 27:1; 37:39;
Isa. 12:2; 25:9

1. How does Paul relate law to grace?

2. What was Isaiah's conviction?

Note, too, that the one – a changed lifestyle – always follow the other – salvation. The God who redeems people anticipates and longs for them to be His people. Those who follow Jesus become His disciples and walk in His footsteps. Those who claim to be born of the Spirit walk in the Spirit. Listen to how the apostle Paul puts it in one of his epistles: 'We died to sin; how can we live in it any longer?' (Rom. 6:2). Further, it was with the giving of the law that the covenant made between God and His people was formally sealed (Exod. 24). The covenant was made possible when a moral God had informed a redeemed people that to deepen their relationship with Him, a lifestyle change follows. Fundamentally, life is about a living, active relationship with God, and these Ten Words put God first.

Scripture has a profound doctrine of ethics, just as it has a profound doctrine of salvation. And nowhere is the relationship between works and salvation more clearly seen and more effectively illustrated than in the timing of the Ten Commandments.

Father, just as I own up to being Yours, help me to own up to all that goes along with being Your disciple – especially Your way of living. Search me and see if there is any hidden sin in my heart. Bring it into the light and help me deal with it. In Jesus' name. Amen.

The divine handwriting

FOR READING & MEDITATION – 1 PETER 1:3–16

'But just as he who called you is holy, so be holy in all you do' (v15)

The giving of these Ten Words established in the clearest possible manner that God is a righteous, holy and good God. Although the idea of God as a God of perfection had been implied in such expressions as, 'Who is like you – majestic in holiness…?' (Exod. 15:11), it was not until the giving of the Ten Commandments that the righteous aspect of His character was most clearly seen.

Handwriting, it has been said, is an accurate indication of character. We cannot be absolutely sure about this, because graphology is not regarded as a science – but proceeding on the assumption that our handwriting does say something about us, let me suggest that at Sinai God wrote to humanity in His own handwriting, and an examination of that handwriting reveals an aspect of His character that hitherto had not been clearly seen. From the darkness surrounding the top of Sinai, Moses came down with two tablets of stone on which were inscribed in God's own hand the words of the Ten Commandments (Exod. 32:16). Though there would be other occasions when God would write to humankind, this was the first evidence of His handwriting.

What does it reveal? Has it some vital secret to show us concerning His transcendent character? Most certainly it has! We cannot be saved by trying to keep these Commandments, but they reveal the heart and will of a holy and righteous God – an aspect that needs restating in today's world. They also reveal how a child of God can live a holy life, with God at the centre of their life, in a loving, contented relationship, trusting in Him alone.

FURTHER STUDY

Isa. 6:1–8;
1 Sam. 6:19–20;
Psa. 99:9

1. What did Isaiah hear the seraphs declaring?

2. What did the men of Beth Shemesh ask?

Father, in Your presence I am made over and over again until I am transformed into Your likeness. Help me to spend more time with You, then I will become more like You. In Jesus' name. Amen.

The God who is there

FOR READING & MEDITATION – EXODUS 20:1–17

*'I am the LORD your God, who brought you out of Egypt...
You shall have no other gods before me.' (vv2–3)*

We are ready now to begin the task of exploring one by one each of the Ten Commandments. It is interesting to note that they begin, not with a prohibition – 'you shall not' – but with an affirmation: 'I am the LORD your God, who brought you out of Egypt...' Before we are given a single Word, God takes the time to tell us who He is. This very first Commandment – that we are to have no other gods – is rooted in two great truths: first, who God is, and second, what God has done.

Let's look first at who God is: 'I am the LORD your God.' There is deep significance in the name by which God reveals Himself here. The Hebrew word for 'LORD' here is Jehovah and the Hebrew word for 'God' is Elohim. The meaning behind the name Jehovah is: 'He that is, He that was, and He that will be.' His very name brings us into the presence of the self-existent God who is because He is. Cast your minds back into the infinite eternity of the past: God says, 'I am He that was.' Stretch your mind into the infinite eternity of the future: God says, 'I am He that will be.' Focus your mind on all that is going on around you at this present moment: God says, 'I am He that is.' The word Elohim means the creator, the ruler of the universe.

FURTHER STUDY

Psa. 96:1–9;
Deut. 26:9–10;
1 Chron. 16:9;
Psa. 95:6

1. What is worship?

2. How does it relate to Lordship?

These opening words and introduction provide both context and motivation. Before the first Word is given God gives us His name and says in effect: I am not just the creator but the one who reveals Himself to my people. At this moment, pause quietly and consider this encouraging and reassuring revelation: what He is He was, and what He was He is, and what He is and was, He ever will be.

Father, let the wonder of this thrilling truth take a firm hold on my spirit today. Others may fail me but You – never. You will always be there! I am eternally grateful. Amen.

Salvation to precede service

FOR READING & MEDITATION – ROMANS 11:33–36; 12:1–13

*'Therefore, I urge you, brothers, in view of God's mercy,
to offer your bodies as living sacrifices' (v1)*

We said yesterday that the first Commandment is rooted in two truths: who God is and what He has done. Yesterday we looked briefly at the first of those factors – who God is (Jehovah Elohim). Today we look at the second – what He has done: 'I am the LORD your God, who brought you out of Egypt, out of the land of slavery' (Exod. 20:1).

I referred earlier to the fact that the Ten Commandments were given to the children of Israel *after* their exodus from Egypt, not before it. The reason for this is because (as we saw) we are saved *from* something before we can be saved *for* something. This truth is portrayed everywhere in the Scriptures. Bible commentators often emphasise that almost every scripture passage that contains laws or ethical guidelines is preceded by a section on the doctrine of salvation and deliverance. One commentator suggests these are guidelines for responding gratefully to the grace of God, who loves and saves His people before they do anything at all. Remember, these Ten Words are given *after* the context of a dramatic deliverance from slavery. The book of Romans is another example of this. The first 11 chapters of Romans explain and expound the plan of salvation and then in chapter 12 Paul urges us to respond to this truth in sacrificial living. Why are we being urged? It is because of the kind of God we have and what He has done for us. Then follow four chapters of ethical lifestyle and principles of conduct.

Understanding who God is and what He has done is essential to comprehending the reason for the Ten Commandments. He is the one who reveals and reaches out to save.

FURTHER STUDY

1 Chron. 29:1–5;
Exod. 32:29;
Prov. 23:26

1. What question did David ask concerning the building of the Temple?

2. What does 'consecrate' mean?

God, whenever I feel challenged by the things You ask me to do, help me to remember the things that You have done for me, to really know you as the one who first and foremost loves and saves His people. In Jesus' name. Amen.

All life is worship

FOR READING & MEDITATION – EXODUS 34:1–14

'Do not worship any other god, for the LORD, whose name is Jealous, is a jealous God.' (v14)

We continue looking at the fact that when giving the Ten Commandments, God first establishes His place in our lives: 'I am the LORD your God.' Then He gives the command: 'You shall have no other gods before me.' This statement was made at a time and context when people believed in many gods. Here God has introduced and established Himself in such a way as to make the other gods non-existent and irrelevant. He is Jehovah Elohim.

Dr G. Campbell Morgan says of this first Commandment:

FURTHER STUDY

Lev. 26:1–13;
Exod. 20:4;
Deut. 7:25;
11:16–17

1. What are the rewards of obedience?

2. What are the results of idolatry?

'Every man needs a god. There is no man who has not, somewhere in his heart, in his life, in the essentials of his being, a shrine in which is a deity whom he worships.' All life is worship. It is as impossible for a person to live without an object of worship as it is for a fish to exist out of water. There may be a false god at the centre of one's life, but every activity of being, every energy of the personality, everything to which we give our energy – all these things are worship. However worthy or unworthy, the thing to which an individual gives his or her ultimate devotion is the god of that person's life. Since mankind's fall into sin in the Garden of Eden, their inclination is to choose a substitute god to worship instead of the true God.

In order to function on this earth, we all inevitably look to something beyond ourselves. And that 'something' helps us make choices in life; it gives us a set of values or priorities that guide us and influence all our decisions. We have little choice as to whether or not we will worship, but we have a lot of choice about what or whom we will worship; may we, through God's grace working within us, make the right choice (see Josh. 24:15).

God – invisible yet there – Your Word sets before me a choice as to which god I will worship. I choose You – the true and ever-present one. Establish Yourself even more firmly at the centre of my being. In Jesus' name I pray. Amen.

The dynamic behind idolatry

FOR READING & MEDITATION – JEREMIAH 2:1–13

'But my people have exchanged their Glory for worthless idols.' (v11)

We continue looking at the thought that people inevitably worship something – either the one true God or a god of their own making. This incontrovertible truth reveals the dynamics that lies behind idolatry. When anyone fails to recognise the living God or loses the vision of Him who says, 'I am Jehovah Elohim,' then he or she will put something else in the place of the true God. What the first Commandment is really saying to us is this – let God be God.

Whenever I read the first epistle of John, an epistle in which John has been talking about some of the loftiest concepts in Christianity – 'God is love', 'abide in Him', 'we shall be like Him' and so on – I am struck by the apparent anti-climax of the exhortation with which John ends: 'Dear children, keep yourselves from idols' (1 John 5:21). Did John end this great exposition of maturity with an immature ending? Or was it the very pinnacle? I am convinced that John was never more guided of God than when he wrote those words. With profound insight he put his finger on the greatest single hindrance to spiritual maturity – 'idols'.

We usually associate 'idols' with pagan faiths but idols are an expression of a universal tendency – the tendency to put something else in the place of God. Anything that becomes a centre of love and attention – a love and attention greater than the love and attention we give to God – is an idol. Idolatry is really substitution – substitution of the real for the unreal. And idolatry does not have to be an outright resistance to God, or the result of a conscious hostility towards Him; it can be demonstrated by simply relegating Him to irrelevance.

FURTHER STUDY

Rom. 1:18–32; Acts 17:29; Jer. 10:5

1. What was the glory of God exchanged for?
2. What was the result?

Father, help me to see the insidious nature of this shadow called 'idolatry'. Guide me as in Your presence I search my heart, and show me how to 'break down every idol and cast out every foe'. In Jesus' name I pray. Amen.

God has no plural

FOR READING & MEDITATION – DEUTERONOMY 6:1–12

'Hear, O Israel: The LORD our God, the LORD is one.' (v4)

Today I want to put before you the idea that just as we have a need to worship built into our personalities, so also we have a built-in need for only one God. And we do not come to health and fullness in our personalities unless we focus on and worship the one true God.

Elton Trueblood, a twentieth-century American theologian, says that the number 'one' is different from all the other numbers and this fact is caught up and reflected in our language. Singular means one and only one, while plural means more than just one; it means upwards of two. It can be two, three or three million. The man with one wife is essentially different from the man with two wives. The man with two wives is in the same category as the man with four hundred wives. Whether a man has two or two hundred wives, he is totally different from the man with one wife, because he cannot say, 'I love only one.'

FURTHER STUDY

James 1:1–18;
Matt. 6:24;
12:25–30

1. What does double-mindedness bring?

2. What did Jesus say?

Christians have only one God. The word 'gods' is not the plural of the word 'God'. That's why we spell it with a small 'g'; God has no plural. When we love God with one part of our being and love some other god with another part of our being, we live in a constant dividedness – and it's hard to arrive at health and wholeness in our personalities. Idolatry, or divided loyalty in the soul, leads to disease in the inner being. Polytheism (many gods) in the heart leads to an increasing tightening tension in the personality. If our loyalty is divided, our personality will be too. I myself am convinced that at the core of what many counsellors and therapists wrestle with is a failure on the part of that person to give himself or herself in absolute surrender to the one true and living God.

Father, I see that Your command to have no other gods before You has within it a concern for my deepest welfare. I can never wholly be what I am designed for unless I give myself wholly to You. Help me understand this. In Jesus' name. Amen.

Is a photograph a sin?

FOR READING & MEDITATION – LEVITICUS 19:1–14

*'Do not turn to idols or make gods of cast metal for yourselves.
I am the LORD your God.' (v4)*

We move on now to examine the second of the Ten Words:
'You shall not make for yourself an idol in the form of anything in heaven above or on the earth beneath or in the waters below. You shall not bow down to them or worship them' (Exod. 20:4–5). At first this might look like a repetition of the first Commandment, but it is much more than that. The first Commandment – namely, 'you shall have no other gods besides the one who makes Himself known by the name Jehovah Elohim' – is concerned with whom we worship while the second is more concerned with how we worship. This instruction was given at a time when images were thought to function as mediators between people and their gods.

First, let's make clear what exactly is being forbidden here. I have known Christian people interpret this Commandment to mean that every form of art is idolatrous. Some who interpret it in this way believe that even having one's photograph taken is a sin, and will not allow a picture or painting to be displayed in their home. Few people would hold to such an interpretation today, but in my own circle of friends and acquaintances I knew of at least two.

This, however, could not have been the divine intention, for immediately after giving the Ten Commandments God gave instructions for His people to make a tabernacle for worship, at the heart of which were images of cherubim and seraphim. It is not a sin to make a representation of something; it is a sin, however, to make that representation the focus of our worship. Aaron may have sought to represent God with the golden calf but, as with all images, it detracted from God's glory and conveyed false ideas about Him.

FURTHER STUDY

1 Cor. 8; 10:14–22; 12:2

1. What did Paul say to the Corinthians about idolatry?

2. How are we to show care for weaker brethren?

Father, show me, in an even deeper way than ever before, the art of true worship. I long to worship You in the way You long to be worshipped – in spirit and in truth. Help me, dear Father. In Jesus' name. Amen.

What about aids to worship?

FOR READING & MEDITATION – PHILIPPIANS 3:1–11

'For it is we... who worship by the Spirit of God, who glory in Christ Jesus, and who put no confidence in the flesh' (v3)

Permit me to once again explain what I think the second Commandment is saying: we are not forbidden to make a representation of things, but we are warned not to make these things the focus of our worship. The force of the Commandment lies in these words: 'You shall not bow down to them or worship them.' Many years ago in Westminster Abbey, London, some statues were removed because people used to burn lamps before them and kneel down and worship them. This was a violation of the second Commandment and the ecclesiastical authorities moved in to stop it.

FURTHER STUDY

John 4:1–26;
Matt. 4:10;
Rev. 14:7

1. What point was the Samaritan woman making when she asked about worship?

2. What did Jesus declare about true worship?

But what about the use of objects like pictures, paintings, crucifixes, as an aid to worship? Some say an object that has sacred associations, such as a painting or a crucifix, helps them to focus on God or Christ and is a useful aid in the act of worship. They are at pains to point out that they do not worship the object but use it to help them think more deeply about spiritual things. I can understand how an object that has spiritual associations triggers off thoughts that lead towards God, but we need to be wary about over reliance on these aids.

Over the years I have talked to many who have told me that for them meaningful worship depends on being in the right place, such as a church or cathedral, and in the presence of the right objects, such as a painting or a crucifix. However, it is the constant presence of the Spirit who will always lead us into a place of worship. Can I encourage you to cast your eyes upon Jesus and look full in His wonderful face, it is then that the things of earth take their right place.

Father, bring me into such a close relationship with You and the Holy Spirit that I will be less and less dependent on the material and more and more aware of the spiritual. In Christ's name I pray. Amen.

Support CWR today!

Our vision is to reach as many people as possible with our life-changing books, resources teaching and training. As a charity, a lot of the work we do is because of the generosity of CWR Partners who help support our work through regular prayer and donations.

If you can, we would love you to become a Partner from as little as 50p a day (£15 per month). Your regular gift will help us to:

· Develop Bible reading notes for future generations
· Send 60,000 vital resources to prisons in the UK and Australia
· Equip church leaders in the developing world with needed resources
· Create digital resources online for young adults to build tomorrow's Church
· Make new, fun, Bible-based resources for children, such as the new *Miniphant & Me* series!

Without our Partners' support, we would be unable to do the work we do, so please consider supporting us and get in touch:
partners@cwr.org.uk
01252 784709

As a Partner, you will receive quarterly newsletters keeping you up to date with our work and any exciting new developments. You will also be invited to attend Partners' Days, where you will hear from guest speakers and the CWR team, followed by a delicious meal.

The 'how'

FOR READING & MEDITATION – JOHN 4:1–26

'the true worshippers will worship the Father in spirit and truth' (v23)

We spend another day exploring the issue we touched on yesterday – the relationship of things, such as sacred objects, ornate services, beautiful and aesthetic surroundings, ritualistic ceremonies and so on, to true worship. In the ancient Tabernacle in the Wilderness, the worship centre of the children of Israel, there were three sections. First, the outer court where everyone could come; second, the inner court where only the priests would gather; third, the holy place into which only the high priest could enter.

FURTHER STUDY

Luke 1:46–55;
1 Thess. 5:23;
Heb. 4:12

1. How did Mary worship the Lord?

2. What did Paul pray for the Thessalonians?

Worship, it seems to me, can be related to three areas of our being: spirit, soul and body. We can worship God with our bodies (the outer court). We can worship Him also in the soul (the inner court). We can worship Him too with our spirits (the holy place). The most authentic worship takes place when we move beyond the realm of the soul (the senses) to where we open our spirit to God's Spirit and we pour out to Him our thanksgiving, our love and our praise. Worship that reaches the deepest part of God's being is worship that flows in response from the deepest part of our being – the spirit.

Let's be careful that our love for the beautiful and the aesthetic does not entice us to stay in the realm of worship where our senses are being stirred (the soul) and we become more concerned about what we are getting out of the act of worship than about what is given to God. The woman at the well wanted to talk with Jesus about where God should be worshipped, but He was more concerned with highlighting and being clear about how we worship. As far as New Testament worship is concerned, the how is more important than the where.

Father, help me in my worship to be more concerned with connecting to You than about having my own senses aroused or stirred. Teach me how to worship You in spirit and in truth. In Jesus' name I ask it. Amen.

A God who brooks no rivals

FOR READING & MEDITATION – DEUTERONOMY 4:15–24

'For the LORD your God is a consuming fire, a jealous God.' (v24)

We continue with our focus on the second Commandment and we come now to the words: 'for I, the LORD your God, am a jealous God' (Exod. 20:5). Many contemporary commentators make a lot out of this statement. They say: 'I can understand a God who redeems and liberates and sets free, but a God who is jealous? Isn't this going too far?'

People may be repelled by the idea of a jealous God, but that is only because they do not fully understand what the Scripture is saying here. The word 'jealous' in the Old Testament has its roots in the same word as 'zealous'. When we say that God is jealous we are really saying that He is full of concern for His redeemed people. It's not so much about intolerance as exclusiveness. Israel had a covenant relationship with God. It was likened to a marriage. He knows that no one can do for them what He can do for them and He pursues their interests with all the zealousness and love of which He is capable. We must not import into the word any suggestion of the feelings we get when we are jealous – resentment, envy, distrust, suspicion, and so on. When the Bible says He is jealous, it means that He is motivated to maintain His good name, bring about the highest good in the lives of His children, and ensure that His people understand who He really is.

FURTHER STUDY

Josh. 24:16–27; 1 Kings 14:22; Deut. 29:20

1. How did Joshua describe the Lord?

2. What was the response of the Israelites?

Think of it this way: God has given Himself fully to us and in return He longs that we might give ourselves fully to Him. This is an expression of mutual love between covenant partners. He wants to look at us and say: 'You are my child; I am totally yours and you are mine.' This kind of jealousy does not deter me; it draws me. A God like this can have my heart any day.

Father, how can I ever sufficiently thank You that Your love is a zealous love. You love me so much that You will brook no rivals. This gives me constant hope and security. I am so deeply, deeply grateful. Thank You, dear Father. Amen.

Love to a thousand generations

FOR READING & MEDITATION – DEUTERONOMY 7:1–16

'he is the faithful God, keeping his covenant of love to a thousand generations of those who love him and keep his commands.' (v9)

We spend one more day on the second Commandment and we look now at the statement: 'I... am a jealous God, punishing the children for the sin of the fathers to the third and fourth generation of those who hate me, but showing love to a thousand generations of those who love me and keep my commandments' (Exod. 20:5-6). These words contain both a warning and a promise, and they are among the most misunderstood words in the Old Testament.

Take first the warning: 'punishing... for the sin of the fathers to the third and fourth generation'. Does this mean that if a man is sinful and impure God will punish his child? No, that is not what it is saying. The plain meaning of these words in context is that if someone worships a representation of God and not the true God Himself, then the consequences of that action will have repercussions down throughout the generations. Anyone who worships something other than the true God sets up influences in his or her family that go on reverberating from generation to generation. Such people risk not only themselves but the children who follow them. Their concept of God and worship is passed on to their children and their children's idea of worship will be passed on to their children – and so on.

FURTHER STUDY

Psa. 112; 145:1–7; 48:12–14

1. What will one generation declare to another?

2. What does the psalmist do every day?

But note the promise standing alongside the warning: 'showing love to a thousand generations of those who love [Him] and keep [His] commandments.' Those who love Him and keep His commandments are more likely to influence the thousandth generation for good. Should we not come before our faithful God and plead with Him again to revive His Church (Psa. 85:6) so that we will have a good influence on succeeding generations?

Father, I am awestruck at the thought that I may influence future generations. Help me to know You and worship You in such a way that others may see a true picture of You in everything I say and do. In Jesus' name I pray. Amen.

What's in a name?

FOR READING & MEDITATION – EXODUS 22:20–31

'Do not blaspheme God or curse the ruler of your people.' (v28)

We turn now to the third of the Ten Words given at Sinai: 'You shall not misuse the name of the LORD your God, for the LORD will not hold anyone guiltless who misuses his name' (Exod. 20:7). A popular view of this Commandment is that it forms a prohibition against using God's name as a swear word, but there is a lot more to it than that. Names are of the utmost importance – they are so much more than just words. The giving of a name is an important moment; much thought and consideration is given to a name. What associations spring to mind when you hear a name – are good feelings associated with it, or sometimes are they not so good?

Very often parents will settle on a name because of its meaning and significance to them. Many names in the Bible are either descriptive of some physical attribute or personality characteristic. Very often it was an indication of something that God was going to do in that person's life or a reflection of God's blessing in the parents' life. Joseph had two sons, the first he named Manasseh, meaning God has made him forget (God had made him forget the troubles in his father's household) and the second, Ephraim, meaning God has made him fruitful in the land of his affliction. People have even changed or been given new names as a result of God's work in their lives. Take for example the patriarchs: in Genesis 17:5 when Abram became Abraham and then in Genesis 32:28 Jacob became Israel. Whenever we meet somebody for the first time we introduce ourselves, most often by first using our name. In the very first Commandment God has introduced Himself by name, which shows us that God is not a something but a someone.

FURTHER STUDY

Rom. 2:17–24;
Isa. 52:5;
Ezek. 20:27

1. How can we dishonour God's name?

2. How can it be avoided?

Father God, help me this day to grasp the wonder of the fact that you have revealed Yourself and Your name to me. I am in awe that I am known by name by the one who created the heavens and the earth. In Jesus' name. Amen.

Use with care

FOR READING & MEDITATION – EZEKIEL 20:30–44

'Go and serve your idols... But afterwards you will surely listen to me and no longer profane my holy name' (v39)

These Ten Words given by God, begin with the God who created the world and made a covenant with His people and then freed them from slavery. The first two Commandments are focused on our response to God in faith and worship, rejecting other gods and listening to and trusting God rather than trying to recreate Him in images of our own making. Because it is such a privilege to know God's name, this third Commandment teaches us to have a reverent attitude to His name and all that His name stands for.

FURTHER STUDY

Matt. 5:33–37;
Lev. 19:12;
James 5:9–12

1. What did Jesus teach?

2. What should 'not be'?

The ancient Jews held God's name in such awe that they wouldn't even pronounce it. Even when writing it, a copyist would take endless pains to make sure he had it right. First, he would bathe and don full Jewish dress. Then he would proceed with the utmost caution, making sure that he had enough ink on his pen to finish writing, for it was regarded as irreverent to dip the pen back in the ink in the middle of writing God's name. It was said that if a king addressed a copyist when he was writing God's name, the copyist would ignore him completely. What a stark contrast to the indifferent attitudes shown towards God's name today.

Those who have studied 'the dynamics of profanity' say that people who sprinkle their conversations with blasphemies to the Deity do so because of a deep insecurity in their personalities. They feel small on the inside and attempt to prop themselves up by linking their own frail personalities to a great and mighty power. However, they do not do it in a humble way, but arrogantly. It is a kind of compensation that says: 'I feel small but I won't admit it and to show how much bigger I am than anyone else, I will bring the Deity down to my size.'

Father, help me to learn respect for Your name. Give me a new vision of all that Your name represents, so that I may treat it with the respect and awe it deserves. In Jesus' name I ask it. Amen.

True reverence

FOR READING & MEDITATION – EZEKIEL 39:1–13

*'I will make known my holy name among my people Israel.
I will no longer let my holy name be profaned' (v7)*

We continue examining the third Commandment, and we look today at the meaning of the word 'profanity'. It comes from the Latin *pro*, which means 'in front of', and *fane*, which means 'the temple'. Those who use profanities take the sacred and the holy out of the temple and allow their hearts, minds and thoughts to become a common marketplace. In other words, they reach up and take that which ought to be treated with awe and respect and drag it down to the level of the commonplace.

Charlton Heston, the famous film star, was once asked in an interview if any of the characters he had played in his religious films had changed his spiritual outlook. He thought for a moment and said: 'Well, you can't walk barefoot down Mount Sinai with the Ten Commandments in your hand and be the same person you were when you went up.' This is so true; you can't spend time in the presence of God, talk to Him in prayer, commune with Him, read His Word and then toss His name around lightly. I confess that at times I struggle when I hear Christians who refer to God in such phrases as 'the man upstairs', 'the one above', 'the great captain in the sky', and so on. I wonder if Moses might have said the same after His revelation on Mount Sinai.

Someone might say: 'Well, what about Romans 8:15, where we are encouraged to call God not just Father but "Daddy"?' This verse says, 'And by him [the Holy Spirit] we cry, "Abba"' (literally 'Daddy'). But I see no conflict, for although the term is familiar, it is not irreverent. The person who knows true reverence knows also that God's name is the doorway to the audience chamber of His heart.

FURTHER STUDY

Neh. 1:1–11;
2 Cor. 7:1;
Rev. 11:18

1. What did Nehemiah delight in?

2. What did Paul encourage the Corinthians to have?

Grant, dear Father, that familiarity with Your name may never cause in me irreverence or disrespect. It is a thin line between legalism and liberalism, but help me walk it. In Jesus' name. Amen.

The worst profanity

FOR READING & MEDITATION – ISAIAH 48:1–11

*'Listen to this... you who take oaths in the name of the LORD...
but not in truth or righteousness.' (v1)*

In Scripture, the name of God is always a revelation. In every new title by which God made Himself known to humans He revealed a new aspect of His character. We learn new truths concerning His nature with each new title by which God makes Himself known. Bearing this in mind, a new ray of light falls on the Commandment: 'You shall not misuse the name of the LORD your God.' When we use the name of God, we use it in a way that is true to its meaning and its intention, and when we fail to do this we misuse His name and fall short of this third Commandment. We honour God's name in actions and speech, and it's been said that the most arrogant profanity is to call yourself a Christian and not live like Christ. This can do untold damage – Mahatma Gandhi reportedly once said: 'I like your Christ, I do not like your Christians. Your Christians are so unlike your Christ.'

FURTHER STUDY

Matt. 5:33–37;
Num. 30:1–2;
Deut. 23:21;
Eccl. 5:4

1. What does it mean to make a vow?

2. How did Jesus illustrate the shallow vow?

This is what happened in today's passage – the people swore by the name of the Lord, but not in truth; they made mention of the name of God, but not in righteousness. They used the name of God, but their lives did not line up with the revelation contained in that name. This, then, is the deep meaning behind the third Commandment – we misuse the name of God when we do not use it in the way God intended it should be used, and when we ourselves are not true to the revelation of God that the name makes. When we say, 'Lord, Lord,' and do not do the things God asks of us, we disrespect His name. His name carries with it a remembrance of all that He has done for His people. If the truth be known, the misuse of God's name in the Church is far more dangerous and damaging than when it is misused in the street.

God, forgive us that we so easily take Your name upon our lips, yet so often fail to live up to all that Your name represents. Help us, dear Father, to bring our lives in line with Your character. For Jesus' sake. Amen.

Your street. Your community.
Your prayers!

We believe that local people praying for their neighbours and community can change lives.

'*People came from surrounding churches and most exciting of all, strangers: students, holiday makers, families, groups of children, old people, migrants, young people on their way home from a night out... so many people all with a story to tell. Thank God for all He is doing with each small prayer!*'

National Prayer Weekend is coming to your street in one week! **It's not too late to get involved...**

Sign up: Commit to pray and place your community pin on the prayer map.

Equip: Use free online resources to plan your weekend, including booklets ideal for introducing people to prayer.

Pray: Ask people in your local area whether they would like prayer. Then gather the prayer requests together and pray – as an individual, with your small group, or get your whole church involved!

Join in with people praying all over the world on 28–30 September and see God move in your community.

Find out more at **www.national-prayer-weekend.com**
Find us and follow us @NPWtogether to connect with other people praying all over the world.

Worship and work

FOR READING & MEDITATION – ISAIAH 56:1–8

'Blessed is the man who does this... keeps the Sabbath without desecrating it' (v2)

Today we focus on the fourth Commandment: 'Remember the Sabbath day by keeping it holy. Six days you shall labour and do all your work, but the seventh day is a Sabbath to the LORD your God' (Exod. 20:8–9). This Commandment is the last and the longest in the first section of the Decalogue – the section that deals with man in his relationship to God. There is a lot of confusion, dogmatism and misunderstanding surrounding this particular Commandment, and so we must move very carefully and prayerfully over these next few days.

FURTHER STUDY

Gen. 1;
Heb. 4:1–11

1. On which day did God create Adam?

2. What was the first day Adam experienced?

The Commandment in its original setting was given to the Hebrew people to establish the regular habit of making the seventh day a day of total rest. It is popularly believed that this fourth Commandment refers only to the Sabbath – but that is not so. Its full meaning can only be understood when we look at the second half of the Commandment, which has to do with the remaining six days. The Commandment consists of two simple injunctions: first, 'Remember the Sabbath day by keeping it holy', and second, 'Six days you shall labour'.

It is the will of God for us that we work, and it is also the will of God that on one day in seven, we focus our whole attention on worship. Work and worship complement one another. The one who never works (this is more about attitude and not life circumstances when one is not able to work) is living an unbalanced life. When we follow this pattern we are restored and blessed. The two parts of the Commandment cannot be separated; they are to be seen as a whole. This is work–life balance in perspective. Work makes for worship, and worship fits and tunes the whole being for work.

Father, help me understand these two important functions – worship and work. Help me balance the relationship of these two things so that I might get the best out of my worship and also out of my work. In Christ's name I ask it. Amen.

True re-creation

FOR READING & MEDITATION – EXODUS 16:11–36

'This is what the LORD commanded: "Tomorrow is to be a day of rest,
a holy Sabbath to the LORD."' (v23)

The idea of the Sabbath was not new to the children of Israel, and as far we know no other nation had this practice, for as we see in today's passage, God had introduced the Sabbath to them prior to the giving of the law on Sinai. The principle of the Sabbath is rooted in the nature of God, for following the six days of creation we read 'on the seventh day he rested from all his work' (Gen. 2:2).

The idea of the Sabbath, or a one-day rest in seven, is often forgotten in this 24/7 technological age, but it was established by our creator for good reason. Every part of our being – spirit, soul and body – is the result of careful consideration and forethought by our maker, and we are more likely to live at our maximum potential when we follow His instructions. We live in a world that contains all that is necessary for our physical being, but it requires energy and effort. The majority of human beings work tirelessly, and often to the neglect of many other priorities and people; but there needs to be balance. If we do not rest we are in danger of literally wearing ourselves out.

There is more, however. God decrees that for one day each week, men and women lay aside the tools of their trades and focus their minds on the worship of their creator. This aspect of the fourth Commandment is misunderstood. People focus on such things as rest and recreation and fail to realise that re-creation is not just a physical thing, it is spiritual also. None of us is really ready to face the challenge of six working days (or even five!) unless we have been spiritually prepared by fully giving ourselves to the worship of God.

FURTHER STUDY

Isa. 58;
Exod. 20:8;
34:21;
Isa. 56:1–2

1. How is joy in the Lord equated to the Sabbath?

2. What is promised to the man who keeps the Sabbath?

Loving heavenly Father, I see that You have established the Sabbath not merely as a holiday, but as a holy day. Help me to see Your divine purposes running through it. For Your own dear name's sake. Amen.

The Lord of the Sabbath

FOR READING & MEDITATION – MATTHEW 12:1–14

'How much more valuable is a man than a sheep!
Therefore it is lawful to do good on the Sabbath.' (v12)

Although the principle of ceasing from all kinds of labour on the seventh day is clearly established in the Old Testament, when we move to the New Testament, we find that we are faced with several conundrums. Although it is clear that Jesus affirmed the spirit of the law of the Sabbath, He appears at times to have broken the letter of it. In other words, He did not hold to it legalistically. When His disciples were criticised for picking some ears of corn and eating them on the Sabbath, Jesus defended their action saying, 'For the Son of Man is Lord of the Sabbath.' Later He Himself healed on the Sabbath day and this so incensed the law makers that they went away and plotted to kill him. The healing at the Pool of Bethesda was, you may remember, done on the Sabbath day and John tells us that as far as the letter of the law was concerned (in the eyes of the Jews), Jesus had clearly broken the Sabbath (see John 5:18).

FURTHER STUDY

John 7:14–24;
9:14;
Mark 6:1–6

1. What did Jesus say of the Sabbath?

2. How did the people of Nazareth react to the teaching Jesus gave on the Sabbath?

Interestingly, when we step into the New Testament we find that the fourth Commandment of these Ten Words is the only Commandment not to be repeated there. All the other Old Testament Commandments are reiterated and their spiritual meaning explained in the pages of the New Testament, but not the one concerning the Sabbath. In all the lists of the New Testament, Sabbath-breaking is never mentioned, while in Galatians 4:10–11 and Colossians 2:16–17 Paul clearly warns against a legalistic view of the Sabbath.

Does this mean that since New Testament times the keeping of the Sabbath is no longer important? Is the fourth Commandment no longer applicable? We shall see over the next two days.

Father, I see now why there is so much confusion over this important matter of the Sabbath. Help me to think this through with You so that I come out, not under law, but as a loving and obedient disciple. In Jesus' name I ask it. Amen.

From Saturday to Sunday

FOR READING & MEDITATION – JOHN 20:1–19

'Early on the first day of the week... Mary Magdalene went to the tomb and saw that the stone had been removed' (v1)

Before tackling the issues we faced yesterday concerning the keeping of the Sabbath, we ask the question why it is that most of the Christian Church keeps Sunday rather than Saturday as the Sabbath. The Early Church stopped celebrating Saturday Sabbath and instead began keeping the first day of the week (our Sunday) because that was the day on which Christ rose from the dead. This was done with the approval and authority of the apostles, Christ's appointed teachers. In 1 Corinthians 15 Paul talks about the great theme of the resurrection, and then follows it in chapter 16:2 with these words: 'On the first day of every week, each one of you should set aside a sum of money in keeping with his income'. In Revelation 1:10, John writes: 'On the Lord's Day I was in the Spirit, and I heard behind me a loud voice'. What a beautiful way to describe the day of rest – 'the Lord's Day'. Personally, I much prefer this to 'Sunday', or even to the word 'Sabbath'.

In the action of changing the Sabbath from Saturday to Sunday in celebration of the resurrection of Jesus, the Early Church swept aside the legalism that was attached to it, while still keeping the principle that lay behind it. That principle – that one day in seven be hallowed and set apart for worship – can never be repealed, for it is rooted in the nature of God, in human nature and in the nature of the universe itself.

So although the day has changed, the Sabbath principle has not. 'The Lord's Day' is still His gift to us – a day set apart, a day of rest and worship, a day of recuperation, re-creation and joy.

Loving heavenly Father, while, in a sense, every day is Your day, help me to understand and experience the specialness that You reserve for me in 'The Lord's Day'. This I ask in Christ's peerless and precious name. Amen.

FURTHER STUDY

Rom. 14;
Eph. 2:11–16;
Col. 2:13–14

1. What was Paul teaching in Romans 14?

2. What will each of us be required to do before God?

Remember

FOR READING & MEDITATION – PSALM 105:1–11

*'Remember the wonders he has done, his miracles,
and the judgments he pronounced' (v5)*

We saw yesterday that although the Early Church changed the Sabbath from a Saturday to a Sunday, they still kept to the principle of refraining from work, where possible, and giving themselves to the corporate worship of God.

Two main principles underlie the Sabbath – rest and remembrance. The fact that we need to rest one day in seven is a principle that has been shown to be physically and psychologically sound. The body of evidence and information now available concerning the importance of rest, recuperation, and work–life balance, and the consequences of not taking time to rest is almost overwhelming. It can have a devastating impact upon our physical and mental health. It so good when modern medicine catches up with Scripture.

FURTHER STUDY

Jonah 2:2–9;
Psa. 63:6;
Eccl. 12:1;
1 Cor. 11:17–32

1. What jogged Jonah's memory?

2. What is a focus for remembrance?

But there is more to a biblical understanding of Sunday than just rest – there is also remembrance. In Deuteronomy 5:15 God follows the command to observe the Sabbath with these words: 'Remember that you were slaves in Egypt and that the LORD your God brought you out of there with a mighty hand and an outstretched arm.' In effect, He was saying: 'You were slaves but you have been delivered. Keep one day in seven holy and remember.' Why remember? Because our sinful nature makes it easy for us to forget. No Sunday ought to pass without our giving some time to remembering how we have been saved from sin and brought out of the world. Remembrance need not be the whole focus, but it ought to be given some focus. If we forget that we were delivered from sin by the Saviour's efforts and not our own, we might soon find ourselves being drawn back to it.

Father, I see clearly now what Sunday means – rest and remembrance. Help me from this day forward to carry these two principles with me into this coming Sunday and every Sunday. In Jesus' name. Amen.

God's plan for the family

'"*Honour your father and mother*" – *which is the first commandment with a promise*' (v2)

The fifth Commandment, which we are about to explore, falls in the second section of the Ten Words – the section that focuses not so much on our relationship to God as on our relationship to each other. Some consider this Commandment to be the bridge between the two sections. Some maintain that the first four Commandments were written on the first tablet of stone, and the last six on the second. We cannot be sure about this, but what we can be sure about is that the six Commandments in this section reveal for all time the divine thinking on human relationships. First comes the family relationship: 'Honour your father and your mother, so that you may live long in the land the LORD your God is giving you' (Exod. 20:12). Families are part of God's plan. Listen to how the AMPC Bible translates Psalm 68:6 like this: 'God places the solitary in families and gives the desolate a home in which to dwell.'

The nature of human life on this earth is that each new generation begins where the last one leaves off. That's not just an interesting theory; it is an indisputable fact. The blessings and sins of one generation have an impact on succeeding generations. This is true physiologically, psychologically and spiritually. And because this is the nature of human society, we need instructions that address the issues and give us clear guidelines on how to live life well.

No nation can rise higher than its homes and families. Indeed, I will go further – no nation can survive unless it gives attention to the principles of effective family living. We either heed the helm or we must heed the rocks.

FURTHER STUDY

Luke 2:39–52;
Lev. 19:3;
Prov. 4:1; 30:17;
John 19:25–27

1. What did Luke say of the boy Jesus?

2. How did Jesus show honour for His mother?

Gracious and loving God, help me to light a flame of honour to Your name that the next generation may get from me and my family a torch that will never go out. In Jesus' name I ask it. Amen.

'Lover, lawgiver and provider'

FOR READING & MEDITATION – PROVERBS 22:1–12

'Train a child in the way he should go, and when he is old he will not turn from it.' (v6)

The fifth Commandment – 'Honour your father and your mother' – is closely linked in thought and intention to those that have preceded it and I wonder if the thought and implication is that the parent is in the place of God to the child. Let me unpack this a little more. In the early days of childhood development, when the child is unable to grasp the most elementary ideas about God, basic truths concerning Him are impressed upon and revealed to the child through what the child sees and hears in his or her parents. Although, in the final sense, God is the creator of all life, in the procession of events, a child owes its being and existence to its parents. And from a vast amount of research it is clear that the attitude of a child towards its parents is quite different from its attitude towards others. What God is to the adult, the parent is to the child – lover, lawgiver and provider.

FURTHER STUDY

Deut. 6:1–7;
Eph. 6:4;
Isa. 38:19

1. When are parents to talk to children about the things of God?

2. What are fathers to do?

A child's response to their parents is often the foundation on which that person will later relate to God. Someone has put it like this: 'Mother and Father are the skylight through which a child gets his or her first glimpse of God.' It is also a sobering thought that the children in the home catch the attitudes of the parents rather than their sayings. The child is like the subconscious mind – it learns by what it sees them doing, rather than by what they say.

The majority of the children of Israel did not enter the promised land because they did not honour or believe God's Word. When we learn to honour our parents, we learn to honour those in authority, and this way we learn to honour God.

Father, help us to live in such a way that the generation following us, especially our families, will have a desire to move in the direction of Your will. Amen.

A flame of devotion

FOR READING & MEDITATION – PSALM 127:1–5

*'Sons are a heritage [assignment] from the LORD,
children a reward from him.' (v3)*

Before going into some of the background of why God instructs us to honour our parents, we spend another day reflecting on the importance of the parent–child relationship. We are doing this because, as we said yesterday, the fifth Commandment is closely linked to those that have preceded it. The implication is that a parent is in the place of God to the child. We also suggested yesterday that in the home children catch the attitudes of parents rather than their words or sayings.

It is attitudes, not just words, that make the deepest impact on the hearts and minds of our children. A scripture that became significant to me on my seventieth birthday was Psalm 71:17–18: 'Since my youth, O God, you have taught me, and to this day I declare your marvellous deeds. Even when I am old and grey, do not forsake me, O God, till I declare your power to the next generation, your might to all who are to come.' I felt challenged to write down those things I had learnt from God over the years that they might be, hopefully, of some use to the following generation. They became the basis of my book *Seven Laws for Life*.

My father put a torch in my hands when I was but a boy, although he did not realise he had done so. The shadow of financial calamity was upon my home in Wales as a result of the miners' strike in the late 1930s. Going upstairs one night, I heard a muffled voice. I stopped and heard my father in heart-breaking prayer. I saw through the little crack in the door more than just a person kneeling in prayer – I saw a flame of pure devotion. I took a wick from that lamp of devotion that night and it has lighted me down the years.

FURTHER STUDY

Gen. 48;
Prov. 20:11;
23:22

1. What are a parent's priorities?

2. What practical steps must be taken to accomplish these?

Gracious and loving heavenly Father, make us worthy of the heritage that has been passed on to us, and may we worthily give it to the age through which we are passing – an age so desperately in need of just this. In Jesus' name. Amen.

Honour

FOR READING & MEDITATION – COLOSSIANS 3:1–17

'Forgive as the Lord forgave you.' (v13)

It is often thought and interpreted that the command: 'Honour your father and your mother,' is addressed only to young children. It is not. This false idea is compounded by confusing the word 'honour' with 'obey'. While the word 'honour' contains the thought of obedience, it is much wider in meaning. To 'honour' means 'to attach weight to; to put in the place of high importance; to reverence and respect'. Honour does not necessarily mean obedience.

For some children, the day may come – after they have got married, for example – when they may disobey a wish of their parents because it is not in the best interests of their partner. But though the day may come when we are no longer required to obey our parents, the day never comes when we are no longer to honour them. When we are young, we honour our parents by obeying them, but when we go out into life and are free to make our own decisions, then honour takes a new form – that of kindness, courtesy and respect.

But what if a parent has been cruel, difficult, indifferent or abusive? This becomes a very real challenge and I want to suggest, if this is you, that you ask God today to begin the well-worn path of forgiveness. I suggest this for your benefit, not for those who may have wronged you. With God's help you can, but it may take time and be a painful journey. Can I suggest that one place to start is to reflect on how much God has forgiven you. Think of the hurt you brought to the heart of God – yet He has forgiven you. Then let the wonder of how much you have been forgiven flow out in forgiveness to your parents.

FURTHER STUDY

Luke 17:1–6;
Mark 11:25;
Eph. 4:32

1. What did Jesus teach about forgiveness?

2. Is there a family member you need to forgive?

Lord Jesus Christ, help me now to forgive those who have wronged me and hurt me. For Your own dear name's sake. Amen.

For more on the often painful subject of forgiveness, see Ron Kallmier and Sheila Jacobs, *Insight into Forgiveness* (Farnham: CWR, 2008).

Character and honour

FOR READING & MEDITATION – DEUTERONOMY 11:8–21

*'Observe therefore all the commands I am giving you today...
so that you may live long in the land' (vv8–9)*

We saw yesterday that the command: 'Honour your father and your mother' has a broad application: not just the period of childhood, but follows on into adult life. We saw also that to honour means much more than obey, although the thought of obedience is contained in the word 'honour'.

Today we ask ourselves: why is the command to honour one's parents coupled with the promise of long life? I believe it is because the honouring of one's parents results in the development of character and lifestyle habits that contribute to the lengthening of one's days. Character moulded in the atmosphere of honour to one's parents has within it the elements of spiritual life that contribute to good physical health and longevity. On the other hand, character formed in the atmosphere of rebelliousness, disobedience, insubordination, and disrespect has within it the elements of recklessness and agitation – all of which contribute to the shortening of life. Our attitudes, it must be remembered, are as important to our physical functioning as are our arteries. One commentator claims that the last six Commandments are all related to and included in the fifth: children who honour their parents will be much less likely to get involved in murder, impurity, theft, slander and covetousness.

FURTHER STUDY

2 Tim. 1:1–7;
Deut. 4:9; 31:13;
2 Chron. 17:3;
26:4

1. What was Paul persuaded of?

2. Why was the Lord with Jehoshaphat?

Let every single one of us take this to heart today and pray and do what we can to preserve and practice the decree that God has given: 'Honour your father and your mother.' And let every mother and father remember that in the plan and purpose of God children get their first glimpse of Him, not just through what their parents say, but through what they do.

Father, as home and family life continue to be assailed from many directions, give me a new vision of what I can do to preserve and practice the truth of Your Word. Hold me together, so that I may hold others together. In Jesus' name. Amen.

The man behind the mission

Having pioneered as a missionary in China for over 50 years and founded the organisation that now exists as OMF, James Hudson Taylor is one of the most renowned missionaries ever to have walked the earth. In celebration of his life and extraordinary evangelical impact, CWR is working on two exciting releases for this October: a docudrama of Hudson's life, made in conjunction with the Christian Television Association, and a brand-new book authored by Ruth Broomhall. Here, Ruth tells us more about the book...

Ruth – let's start with your interesting link with James Hudson Taylor!
Hudson Taylor is my great-great-uncle. His sister Amelia married Benjamin Broomhall, and they had ten children – Noel, their eighth, was the father of Edwin James, my father.

What have you enjoyed most in researching and writing about Hudson Taylor?
Digging deeper into family history, discovering photos and artefacts I have not seen before. It was really special, for example, to read that Hudson Taylor's mother was nicknamed 'the nightingale'. When my father passed away in 2015, my sister mentioned the nightingale at his bedside – how it sings in the darkness, and as Christians we have hope, even in death. It's been an honour to write this book and share a truly incredible spiritual heritage.

Who will benefit from this book and DVD?
Anyone interested in the power of the living God, in mission, in learning from the lives of the great men and women who

have gone before us. The story is powerful and engaging, and the personal letters and reflections of Hudson Taylor and his family give a real sense of the man behind the mission.

What do you hope readers will gain from learning more about this amazing man?

I have tried to focus on Hudson Taylor's character, and his 'faith abounding'. I think people will be amazed at his strength, resilience, and dedication. But it's how he did it, particularly his faith in a faithful God, that I hope will convey a life-changing sense of the power of a living God.

Are there key lessons that Hudson Taylor's life has taught you?

I have been impacted greatly by his unwavering belief in a faithful God; his strong sense of calling; his perseverance through immense challenge and suffering; his love for China and his deeper love for Christ. Perhaps what has challenged me most though, is how he held eternity in view and released his claim on life here, giving him real freedom. He loved life and people deeply, but he loved God more.

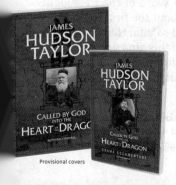

Provisional covers

The book and DVD *James Hudson Taylor: Called by God into the Heart of the Dragon* are available now from Christian bookshops, direct from **www.cwr.org.uk/shop** or by using the order form at the back of these notes.

Book ISBN: 978-1-78259-063-7
DVD EAN: 5027957-001701

The gift of life

FOR READING & MEDITATION – GENESIS 9:1–7

*'Whoever sheds the blood of man, by man shall his blood be shed;
for in the image of God has God made man.' (v6)*

We turn now to consider the sixth Word. This falls within the second group of Commandments which is concerned with our relationships with one another, beginning with the protection of human life expressed as, 'You shall not murder' (Exod. 20:13).

Enshrined within the four words of this Commandment is a fundamental statement about the first principle of life: human existence is sacred. At the very foundation of the social fabric lies the truth of the sovereignty of God over every individual life. And if God regards human life as sacred – we would do well to do so also. Life originates with God and it is His gift to us.

FURTHER STUDY

Gen. 2:1–7;
1 Sam. 2:6;
Job 27:3;
Acts 17:24–26

1. What is it that sustains life?

2. What did Paul declare to the Athenians?

Because God is the originator of life, we can say that human life is a divine creation, marvellous and magnificent in its origin and utterly beyond the comprehension of any human being. Therefore, life is not to be cut off at the hand of someone who does not know or understand all that it contains – its wonder, its meaning, its possibilities. God has a purpose for every individual who enters His world – a purpose stretching far beyond the present moment.

So immense are the issues relating to a person's death that there can be no sin against humanity greater than that of taking life. I say again, this sixth Word of the Decalogue contains a fundamental statement about the first principle of love and life, a statement so clear and so vital that it demands our closest attention – love lies behind this amazing truth. God *is* love, and out of His rich depth of love, God enables life so we can share His love and be in relationship with Him – life is God's gift.

Father, I am so grateful that day by day Your Word is teaching me to look at life from Your perspective. And when my view collides with Yours, help me to be willing to exchange my perspective for Yours. In Jesus' name I ask it. Amen.

Cities of refuge

FOR READING & MEDITATION – NUMBERS 35:6–29

'Six of the towns... will be cities of refuge, to which a person who has killed someone may flee.' (v6)

It is worth noting that although the Authorised Version of the Bible puts the sixth Commandment in this form: 'Thou shalt not kill', almost every other translation uses the word 'murder'. There is good reason for this. The Hebrew word *ratsach*, used in this verse, has a deeper meaning than just to kill; it means to kill in anger or with premeditation. All murder is, of course, killing, but all killing is not necessarily murder.

The passage before us today brings out this point. God instructed Israel to appoint six cities of refuge to which anyone who had been guilty of killing could go and gain protection. The main purpose of these cities was to protect the killer from those who would take it upon themselves to avenge the death of a loved one. Note, however, the criteria which the Scripture gives for differentiating between a killing and a murder. Those who had killed someone but had not intended to do so, were not to be seen as murderers. Those, however, who had killed 'with malice aforethought' (v20) were to be shown no mercy and to be put to death. The task of the 'assembly' (a jury) was to determine whether the killing was intentional or unintentional.

However, unintentional killing was also considered serious. Anyone who took life in this way was denied their liberty for an indefinite term, having to remain in the city of refuge until the death of the high priest. If they ventured from the safety of the protecting walls, he could be slain by the avenger of the one whom he had killed. Life is God's gift and the taking of it, even unintentionally, is a solemn thing. But please notice that God always provides a way of redemption.

FURTHER STUDY

Deut. 16:20;
17:11–13;
Isa. 56:1;
James 2:12–13

1. What are we to maintain?

2. What is linked to justice in the New Testament?

Father, again I ask, impress deeply into my mind the sacredness and importance of everyone I meet today. Help me see those around me from Your point of view. In Jesus' name. Amen.

Made in God's image

FOR READING & MEDITATION – JAMES 3:1–12

'With the tongue we praise our Lord and Father, and with it we curse men, who have been made in God's likeness.' (v9)

We began to see yesterday that murder is such a far-reaching act, not least because we are all made in the image of God; we are what we are by divine love and volition. By bestowing the gift of life, God bestowed the gift of a most wonderful relationship of mankind to Himself. It is important to see that all other relationships grow out of our relationship with God and are subservient to it. We were created first and foremost to be in relationship with God, and out of that rich depth of relationship reach out to those around us. In other words, if we do not have a correct view of our relationship with God, we will not have a correct view of our relationship with one another. Just as night follows day, so those nations who lose their respect and awe of God will in turn lose their respect and awe of each other. Subsequent Commandments dealing with social, civic or blood relationships are binding upon us because they are included within this first and highest relationship of life – our relationship with God.

FURTHER STUDY

Eccl. 2:17–26; 3:1–14; 6:12

1. What did the teacher say is meaningless?

2. What is the gift of God?

One Bible commentator says concerning this sixth Commandment: 'The sacredness of marriage, the right of property, the importance of reputation, the supremacy of character – all gain their force from the nature of life. They mark, in fact, the unfolding of life in all its varied possibilities. The giving of life includes all. The cessation of life ends all.'

In four simple but solemn words, the sixth Commandment throws a binding law around the life of every human life. Everyone has been made in the image of God and is to be deeply loved and deeply respected – from the unformed body in the womb to the grave (Psa. 139:15–16).

God, if only the men and women of this world could see that right relationships with others come only out of a right relationship with You. Help those of us who are Your children to model this truth before their gaze. In Jesus' name. Amen.

A dark and dangerous path

FOR READING & MEDITATION – MATTHEW 5:17–48

'But I tell you: Love your enemies and pray for those who persecute you' (v44)

How, you might wonder, does a person arrive at the place of murder? Let us briefly try to understand the complex set of circumstances surrounding this and see if we can trace what lies behind this devastating and destructive action; how each of us, if not careful, possess the possibility of arriving at such a dark place. More often than not the Scriptures associate hate with murder (1 John 3:15); we also know from our studies that hate develops when anger is not resolved. Joseph became the object of his brothers' anger and hate festered in their hearts and they conspired to kill him.

This is also reflected in the sad and tragic narrative of the two brothers Cain and Abel in Genesis 4:1–16. Cain was angry: anger is almost always preceded by an offence, an event or a blocked goal, which if we do not recognise and resolve will end in anger and frustration. Life in this fallen world offers all manner of opportunities for our expectations not to be met and if we're not careful we can take offence or become angry.

We arrive now at one of the great overarching themes of the Scriptures – forgiveness. What an amazing moment it must have been when, after 20 years of estrangement, Esau embraces Jacob his brother. When we find ourselves in a place of offence, we need to learn to forgive. But 'they are in the wrong' you might say. Well, we don't usually have to forgive someone who is right. It's time to stop, and pause to remember and receive God's grace and forgiveness. Then from that place we can ask God for His help to forgive old offences and not live with anger and frustration, which can take us down dark and dangerous paths.

FURTHER STUDY

Gen. 4:1–16;
1 John 3:11–15;
James 2:8–11

1. Why did Cain murder Abel?

2. Why might favouritism break the sixth Commandment?

Father, help me to understand the full impact of Your forgiveness, grace and unconditional love as if for the very first time. Give me the strength and courage to trust You to work all things together for Your glory. In Jesus' name I pray. Amen.

Are you a murderer?

FOR READING & MEDITATION – MATTHEW 5:17–26

'But I tell you that anyone who is angry with his brother will be subject to judgment.' (v22)

Let's us now consider the roots and motivation of what lies beneath this Commandment. To do that let's focus on the passage before us today, in which Jesus restates the old Commandment, 'Do not murder,' but in doing so He reveals to us the spiritual nature of it. Jesus shows us that the Commandment is not just concerned with the outward blows that would bring about someone's death, rather He takes us to the root of the problem – unrestrained anger in our hearts.

I imagine that very few reading these lines have been involved in the physical act of murder, but how many of us, I wonder, are guilty of murder in the heart? We may not be able to stop anger arising in our hearts, but we can certainly take steps to bring it under control. If we don't, if we allow it to burn and boil within us, we violate the law of love, and in God's sight this makes us as guilty of murder as if we had stabbed someone through the heart with a dagger.

FURTHER STUDY

Psa. 37:1–8;
Prov. 14:17;
Eccl. 7:9;
James 1:19

1. What should we be slow to do?

2. When do we become foolish?

These are solemn words and difficult for many to accept, but the Scripture is crystal clear. In John chapter 8, Jesus, in His dialogue with the Jews, accused them of murderous intent, which led to them taking up stones to kill Him (John 8:31–59). But let the apostle John have the last word: 'Anyone who hates his brother is a murderer, and you know that no murderer has eternal life in him' (1 John 3:15). Once again, we can thank God that out of His great love for His children, He does not wait for us to draw near to Him, but He makes Himself known to us and provides the way of forgiveness and restoration.

Father, in the light of Your Word to me, I ask myself: am I allowing anger against another to abide within my heart? Father, I repent. Forgive me and this day help me to root out every vestige of anger from my heart. In Jesus' name. Amen.

God's first circle

FOR READING & MEDITATION – PROVERBS 14:22–35

'Righteousness exalts a nation, but sin is a disgrace to any people.'
(v34)

We come now to what someone has described as 'the most unpopular Commandment of them all': 'You shall not commit adultery.' It is interesting that immediately following on from the Commandment which declares the sacredness of human life comes the one that declares the sacredness of marriage. It's important to remember that within society, God's first circle is not the nation, not the community, but the family. And within the family circle, His purpose is the intimacy of marriage. Sadly, for many this has become a painful subject. So it is with love and compassion for those who may have been hurt that we explore this difficult issue.

Consider with me again the divine sequence in these Ten Words given by God after the children of Israel's deliverance from Egypt. The first thing that is emphasised is our relationship with God. The second is our relationship with each other. Within this second grouping, the relationship between man and wife is the type and origin of all subsequent relationships. Nothing can be more essential for the social order than the relationship upon which all subsequent ones are built.

Any nation that does not uphold the sacredness of marriage and the unity of the family, and does not resist promiscuity and adultery, is preparing the way, I believe, for its own downfall. The greatness of a people depends upon the purity and moral strength of the people, and every nation that believes the marriage relationship may be disrupted with impunity is sowing the seeds of its own destruction. Unfaithfulness is like dropping a stone in a pond; the ripples don't just stay in the centre – they spread. The effects and consequences can be devastating.

FURTHER STUDY

Heb. 13:1–4;
Prov. 18:22;
Gen. 2:20–25

1. What do husband and wife become?

2. Why is this sacred?

Father, help those who guide our nation to see the damaging effects of unfaithfulness upon the whole of society. Raise up among us strong moral leaders who will give themselves to these concerns. In Jesus' name we ask it. Amen.

Why adultery is so damaging

FOR READING & MEDITATION – PROVERBS 6:20–35

'Can a man walk on hot coals without his feet being scorched?
So is he who sleeps with another man's wife' (vv28–29)

Today we ask ourselves: why is this issue of adultery so sad and destructive in the sight of God? It is because it breaks the unity of the marriage vow, which is a unity designed to illustrate and express the divine image. The unity and intimacy of husband and wife is not subject to human vagary, but is intentional, for 'God created man in His own image… male and female He created them' (Gen. 1:27, NKJ). Although the Bible is clear that being single is God's gift to some people (see Matt. 19:12; 1 Cor. 7:32), marriage between a man and a woman does reflect more fully the oneness in the relationships within the Trinity.

FURTHER STUDY

Matt. 5:27–32;
19:9;
Rom. 7:3;
1 Cor. 6:9–10;
Mark 7:20–21

1. How does Jesus define adultery?

2. What is the consequence of saying yes to adultery?

We discovered earlier, when we looked at the first and second Commandments, that God is passionate that nothing will disrupt or dilute His essential unity. And what He purposes for Himself, He also purposes for us. We are made in His image and adultery and distrust disrupts and destroys the oneness which is designed to be an expression of the divine image. We can hopefully begin to to understand why God is so clear to warn us against this destructive behaviour?

The words of the seventh Commandment are directed against the damage caused by unfaithfulness in marriage – the breaking of the sacred rights of the marriage bond – but its spirit emphatically warns against impurity. Once the idea is accepted that marriage reflects the unity and oneness of the divine image, then it becomes clear that sex prior to marriage is not how God originally designed it to be. I know this may sound out of sync with some, but it is not out of sync with the Bible, God's ultimate life manual.

Father, help me to see the devastating damage of sin, for only then can I understand just what it does to my nature and Your heart. Help me know Your way and walk in it – faithfully and loyally. In Jesus' name. Amen.

Where is the emphasis?

FOR READING & MEDITATION – 2 TIMOTHY 2:1–15

'Keep reminding them of these things. Warn them before God' (v14)

God's desire and plan for intimacy in the marriage relationship and with Himself as a reflection of the Trinitarian relationship is key to helping us understand the importance and issues behind this Commandment. However, faithfulness in marriage is under a direct philosophical and theological assault. We live in a society saturated with sex, in which, as one writer put it, 'the media tells us in a thousand and one ways: "You shall lust, in thought and word and deed."' Within the Christian Church itself some are saying of the seventh Commandment: 'This is a good ideal but one that is almost impossible to live up to.'

But the emphasis ought to be not on how high God has set the moral standards, but on the power He provides to enable us to reach up to them. If we fail, it is not because the standards are too high, but because we have not come to Him in utter dependence and drawn from Him the grace and power we need to live life the way He wants us to – a way that helps both us and our families flourish.

Another argument we often hear is this: 'Adultery is not the unpardonable sin – if someone lapses in this area there is always the hope of divine forgiveness.' Yes, of course, there is forgiveness – I would be the first to affirm this, but there are also consequences. Many Christian teachers major on forgiveness (and rightly so) but do not spend as much time making clear the consequences. We must never stop talking about forgiveness, but neither must we stop talking about the damage caused. If we took more time understanding the rippled consequences of adultery, maybe we might not have to spend so much time helping people to find forgiveness for it.

FURTHER STUDY

1 John 2:15–17; Gal. 5:7–15; Rom. 8:5

1. What are the marks of worldliness?

2. What did Paul warn the Galatians?

Father, help us to be as clear about the nature of sin as we are about forgiveness. Remind us, dear Lord, that the awful thing about sin is not that it breaks Your law but that it also breaks Your heart. In Jesus' name I pray. Amen.

God's fences

FOR READING & MEDITATION – 1 CORINTHIANS 13:1–13

'Love does not delight in evil but rejoices with the truth. It always protects, always trusts, always hopes, always perseveres.' (vv6–7)

Let's pause for one moment and remind ourselves of our journey and the context of God giving these Ten Words. They were given after God dramatically delivered His people from Egypt into a new-found freedom and they were given primarily as instruction on how to best live and grow in relationship with God and each other. God, we should remember, is a good Father. If He places fences and boundaries around us they are for our wellbeing and protection, and not to spoil our misguided ideas of fun. A leading Family Law judge said, 'Without being... over-dramatic or alarmist, my prediction would be that the effects of family breakdown on the life of the nation, and ordinary people in this country, will, within the next 20 years, be as marked and as destructive as... global warming. We are experiencing a period of family meltdown whose effects will be as catastrophic as the meltdown of the icecaps.' Indeed, the scholarly articles and research of decades overwhelmingly demonstrate that children living with their married, biological parents consistently have better physical, emotional and academic wellbeing. Once again, social sciences are beginning to catch up with the maker's instructions for life and living. How thankful I am that God not only instructs us how to live, but also provides provision to find a way back when we lose our way. But how much better it would be to guard our families.

These Ten Words given to us on Sinai, not least the seventh, are not to be dismissed, and we need to pray, teach in our churches, pressure governments and let the world know that when they leap God's fences they endanger not only their own lives, but the lives of many others as well.

FURTHER STUDY

1 Thess. 4:1–8;
Col. 3:5–6;
Eph. 5:3–5

1. What are we to learn?

2. What did Paul write to the Ephesians?

God, help me realise that the lines are being drawn between Your truth and this 'sex-saturated society'. Grant me the wisdom and discernment I need to be a faithful witness to what is right. In Jesus' name. Amen.

FOR READING & MEDITATION – MATTHEW 5:27–48

*'anyone who looks at a woman lustfully has already committed
adultery with her in his heart.' (v28)*

When Jesus restated the seventh Commandment in today's passage, He did with it what He did with the sixth Commandment, 'You shall not murder' – He deepened it and set it in a wider perspective. Once again, He traced the act to its roots – a harboured harmful thought.

Notice I say 'harboured thought', for there is a huge difference between a thought that pops into the head and one that is allowed to remain there. Many married men and women (and single people too) may surprisingly find themselves momentarily caught with unhealthy thoughts concerning someone to whom they are not married. Is the thought sin? I have no hesitation in saying that at that stage it is not. It becomes sin when the self welcomes it, adopts it, owns it and nurtures it. At that stage the thought passes into lust, and it is then that adultery is committed in the heart. A person's inability or fearfulness to turn the desire into a deed is irrelevant to the question of morality. When someone identifies with the desire, it is then that a sin has been committed. It all happens in the mind and will. This is how Jesus shows us that the seventh Commandment can be broken inwardly, even if we do not commit the act of adultery.

FURTHER STUDY

James 1:12–15;
Matt. 15:19;
Titus 1:15–16;
Phil. 4:8

1. Where is sin conceived?

2. What are we to think about?

However, let me remind those of you who may often be tempted in this way that although Jesus carries the moral tests into the deep recesses of the soul, He gives grace to pass them too. He throws His light into darkness within, and yet He does not spurn us. He is faithful and won't let us be tempted beyond what we can bear, and will always provide a way out (1 Cor. 10:13).

Father, I am so thankful for the reminder that in the moment of temptation You are there, not to spurn me but to save me. Your promise is that my mind can be transformed. I give You my thoughts for that process to begin. Help me. In Jesus' name. Amen.

Inverting the order

FOR READING & MEDITATION – ROMANS 2:17–29

'You who preach against stealing, do you steal?' (v21)

We look now at the eighth Commandment: 'You shall not steal' (Exod. 20:15). In some ways this Commandment (as well as the two following it) is of lesser importance than the preceding ones, for these reasons: first, because, as Jesus said, life is more than possessions (Matt. 6:25), and up to this point the Commandments have focused on issues that interfere with our relationship to God or harm human life itself. Second, because breaking the first seven Commandments incurred the death penalty, and this was not so with regard to the last three. But please be careful that you do not misunderstand what I am saying here. Though, for the reasons I have given, they are of lesser importance, that does not mean the last three Commandments are of no importance.

The thing that interests me about contemporary society is the way it has inverted the order of importance of the Commandments. In almost every society in the world, the laws and principles governing stealing rank higher in public opinion than laws and principles that govern our relationship to God. It would certainly be wrong for a man or woman to be punished for refusing to worship, or for worshipping gods other than the true God, but it is an indication of where our society has come to when we are prioritising possessions over people. Ignoring God, misusing His name, defaming His character, denying His existence – public opinion, generally speaking, would not regard any of these as troublesome. It's a subtle thing to disregard God to an annoying irrelevance and this is shown most clearly in the way public opinion has inverted the order of the Ten Commandments.

FURTHER STUDY

Titus 2:9–15;
Prov. 20:10;
Eph. 4:28;
1 Pet. 4:12–17

1. What was Titus to teach the slaves?

2. What are Christians to be known for?

Father, help me always to remember that worship and my relationship with You is a matter of supreme importance. Give me grace to place the emphasis where You place it. In Jesus' name. Amen.

Trust in God

FOR READING & MEDITATION – ROMANS 7:14–25

*'Who will rescue me from this body of death? Thanks be to God –
through Jesus Christ our Lord!' (vv24–25)*

We ended yesterday with the thought that, generally speaking, public opinion is more concerned with the violation of human rights than with the violation of divine rights, and that stealing is seen to be a greater sin than resisting or making God irrelevant. This highlights how society has inverted the Ten Commandments in terms of their order of importance.

A minister once told me that whenever he spoke out against such things as murder, adultery, impurity, theft or lying, he carried his audience with him, but whenever he focused their attention on the more subtle issues of godlessness (a failure to let God be God), he lost their attention. Why is this? I think it is because when we sit in church and hear about sin as murder, lying, stealing, cheating and adultery, most of us can say to ourselves, 'I am not guilty of any of these.' But when the sin of godlessness is identified, who can stand up and say, 'In every area of my life am I letting God be God'? It is perilously easy to get worked up about other people's sin (especially if we know we haven't fallen in that area of life) because it diverts attention from the unconscious sins (a failure to let God be God, for example) that may be going on deep down within our hearts.

FURTHER STUDY

Matt. 23:13–18;
2 Tim. 3:5;
James 1:26

1. What is pharisaism?

2. What is a danger for all of us?

This Commandment at its heart tackles the thorny and troublesome issue of trust in God. Simply, when we trust God, His character and His provision, the need to take matters into our own hands and take what is not ours or more than we need is diminished, as we know we can trust Him to meet our needs. There is nothing that our human nature dislikes and resists more than the thought of dependency.

Father, give me a new vision of Your faithfulness and help me, like the children of Israel, to trust You each day for sufficient manna and daily provision that only You can provide. In Jesus' name I ask it. Amen.

Love and work

FOR READING & MEDITATION – EPHESIANS 4:17–32

'He who has been stealing must steal no longer, but must work, doing something useful with his own hands' (v28)

The Commandment, 'You shall not steal,' is probably one of the most clear-cut of all the Ten Commandments. To steal means to take something which rightfully belongs to someone else. Sociologists agree that this Commandment is probably the most universal of all the laws in the world. In even the most primitive cultures the prohibitions against stealing are of the highest importance. Just as the sixth Commandment ('You shall not murder') safeguards life, and the seventh Commandment ('You shall not commit adultery') safeguards marriage, this eighth Commandment safeguards a person's property and possessions.

FURTHER STUDY

2 Thess. 3:6–14;
Prov. 10:4; 13:4;
Deut. 25:15

1. What rule did Paul give to the Thessalonians?

2. What is the result of laziness?

It has also been recognised that there are only three ways we can come into possession of something: as a free gift from another person, by inheritance, for example; in payment for work done; and as the result of theft. The Scripture recognises the first two and forbids the third. The first two are based upon the essential laws of human interrelationships – love and work. The gift bestowed upon one person by another is an expression of love and becomes the property of the one to whom it is given. Property or possessions purchased from the rewards of toil and work have also been acquired legitimately. But theft breaks with these two important laws of love and work. The thief cannot love the person from whom he steals, and when the law of love is broken they also break the law of work by attempting to possess without toil.

The eighth Commandment recognises the true rights to property, and forbids the possession of anything save upon the condition of obedience to the laws of love and work.

Father, I see that Your school is sensible and the end is always our salvation. Your guidance, however uncompromising, leads to a full life. Help us not to chafe at them but to embrace them as friends. For all Your laws are love. I am so thankful. Amen.

Time to rest, think and be

Leave behind the busyness of life, and take time to be still with God on a CWR residential course in the beautiful surroundings of Waverley Abbey House in Surrey.

Bible Discovery Weekend

Take a much closer look at the Bible and grasp more of the wonder of God's story with in-depth teaching.

'Great to share ideas, listen to the experience of others and have the opportunity to ask questions.'

Introduction to Biblical Care and Counselling

An introductory course designed for those looking to provide pastoral support and care to others.

'I loved all aspects of the course, especially the closeness of the tutors and fellowship of other Christians.'

Inspiring Women Weekends

Times of fellowship and teaching for women of all ages and walks of life, with the opportunity to retreat and rest in God's presence.

'Teaching, worship, fellowship and a strong sense of the presence of God. And what beautiful, peaceful surroundings to do all this!'

To find out more about these courses, and the full range of CWR residential courses, visit **www.cwr.org.uk/courses**

Gaining a clear conscience

FOR READING & MEDITATION – 1 TIMOTHY 1:12–20

'fight the good fight, holding on to faith and a good conscience.'
(vv18–19)

There can be little doubt, like so many of the other Commandments, the eighth Commandment: 'You shall not steal,' is being widely ignored in today's world. Let me re-inforce the thought expressed a few days ago: this instruction has at its heart trust. Can I trust God to supply and meet my needs? Almost daily, the media reports on the latest scam or what is termed 'white collar crime' – crime committed by those who work in the areas of high finance.

Perhaps you are saying at this moment: 'Well, this may be so, but Christians don't need to be reminded about this issue.' Well, have you ever noticed how often the New Testament talks about the subject of money and stealing? Why do you think that is? Mainly it is because stealing is a form of temptation that many Christians wrestle with. Many ministers and counsellors who have had long experience of dealing with people, will tell you that this is quite high up on the list. One minister says: 'I find stealing an increasingly common thing to be confessed at the altar or in the counselling room.' In one particular seminar I used to conduct on the subject 'Gaining a Transparent Conscience', one of the questions I asked people to face was this: have I stolen anything from anyone and not confessed it? And many present would confess to this. Permit me to ask you the same question now: have you broken this eighth Commandment? Expose your heart to the Holy Spirit, let Him identify areas, and then guide you to the steps you need to take to gain a transparent conscience. Give yourself afresh to God today. You can trust Him even in the wilderness to meet with you and be your provision for today.

FURTHER STUDY

Acts 24:10–16;
Rom. 9:1;
2 Cor. 1:12;
Heb. 9:14

1. What was Paul's testimony?

2. Is your conscience clear?

Father, help me to be open and honest. Give me the courage to put right any violations of Your commandments that Your Holy Spirit reveals to me. Give me this day the courage to trust You for today and every day. In Jesus' name I pray. Amen.

Time, treasure and talent

FOR READING & MEDITATION – MALACHI 3:6–18

'Will a man rob God? Yet you rob me. But you ask, "How do we rob you?" In tithes and offerings.' (v8)

It is surprising how easy it is to break the eighth Commandment, 'You shall not steal,' without realising it. If we aren't careful, we rationalise it with euphemisms like 'driving a hard bargain', 'business acumen' or 'a good business deal'. We do it also when we borrow books and never return them, exploit an advantage or fail to make an honest income tax return. The story of Zacchaeus (Luke 19:1–10) shows that we may never know the full joy of our sins being forgiven until we confess and right some wrongs in this area of our lives.

The human desire to take short cuts formed the basis of the three temptations of Jesus in the wilderness (Matt. 4:1–11). Moreover, many other things besides property and possessions can be stolen – a person's honour and good name, for example.

But what about stealing from God? We steal from Him when we fail to fulfil our responsibilities as stewards of time, treasure and talent. Take the matter of treasure as an example – are we stealing from God by keeping for ourselves that which belongs to Him? Listen again to what He said to ancient Israel: 'Will a man rob God?' The problem here was that the Israelites held back their tithes and offerings. Perhaps you might say, 'Tithing is an Old Testament principle; it doesn't apply today.' What does apply, however, is the principle of proportionate giving. And the amount is something people need to continually review and give to God out of a full and thankful heart (see for example Paul's instruction in 1 Cor. 16:1–2 and 2 Cor. 9:7). We know we are not to take that which belongs to another. So what about when that other is God?

FURTHER STUDY

Gen. 14:18–20;
28:22;
Lev. 27:30;
2 Cor. 9:7

1. Who is Melchizedek a type of?

2. What does the Lord love?

Father, help me to stand before You today with an open face and an open being. Save me from all rationalisations. If I have withheld from You – forgive me. Show me how to be a good steward of my time, treasure and talent. In Jesus' name. Amen.

Character and reputation

FOR READING & MEDITATION – PSALM 27:1–14

'false witnesses rise up against me' (v12)

We come now to the last but one of God's Ten Words: 'You shall not give false testimony against your neighbour' (Exod. 20:16). The implications of this Commandment are wide and far reaching, but the major principle underlying it is honesty. When we are open and honest we are free to enjoy stronger relationships – not only with God but with all those we come into contact with every day. It keeps us free from the increasingly tangled webs that lies and deceit spin. Equally, it not only safeguards your reputation but that of others also. God knows that a reputation untarnished is a precious thing, and it is His will and purpose that no one's reputation is stained by a false report.

Reputation can be best understood by comparing it with the word 'character'. Character is what a person is within the depths of their being; reputation is the estimate that other people form of them. A person with a good character can have a bad reputation because of false reports.

Christians have suffered from this and I suspect many reading these lines are in that position now. If so, then let me encourage you. Jesus knows exactly how you feel, for He was rushed to the cross on the basis of false witness. None knows more than He the weight and burden of this sin, for Scripture says of Him: 'He was despised and rejected by men, a man of sorrows, and familiar with suffering' (Isa. 53:3). So close does He come to tormented hearts in these times that a new courage is created within their souls enabling them to stand tall in the midst of discouragement. God's care for the reputation of His children is such that in time – His time – He will fully justify and vindicate them.

FURTHER STUDY

Psa. 101;
Exod. 23:1;
Prov. 12:17;
25:18

1. What was the psalmist committed to?

2. What is a false witness likened to?

Father, help me to take care of my character and trust You to take care of my reputation. And when false reports are given, give me the grace to carry on, knowing that in the end truth will always be justified. In Jesus' name. Amen.

Designed for truth

FOR READING & MEDITATION – JOHN 1:43–51

'Here is a true Israelite, in whom there is nothing false.' (v47)

The words, 'You shall not give false testimony against your neighbour,' demand that any statement made by one person to another, or by one person about another, be in harmony with the truth. As the third Commandment, which warns against misusing of the name of God, lays down the guidelines that our relationship with God should be based on sincerity and truth, so the ninth Commandment instructs us that in our relationships with one another we should be actuated by the same principles.

'God ever deals with man,' says one theologian, 'upon the basis of His full and accurate knowledge of what man is.' In other words, the divine attitude towards men and women is not governed or influenced by the appearances that they might like to present to others, nor by the opinions that others might have of them. God bases His dealings with us on His intimate and accurate knowledge, and that is the way He wants us to deal with others. Listen to these weighty and powerful words taken from the psalmist: 'O LORD, you have searched me and you know me… you perceive my thoughts from afar' (Psa. 139:1–2).

FURTHER STUDY

1 Pet. 3:8–16;
Psa. 34:13;
1 Tim. 5:11–13

1. How can others be made to feel ashamed of their slander?

2. Are you guilty of speaking ill of others?

Now when we step down from the divine level to the human level, we recognise that earthly knowledge is limited, but allowing for those limitations, God requires us as far as is possible to relate to one another in sincerity and in truth. Our whole social fabric rests on the testimony that one person bears in relation to another, and there can be no just society where this is not so. Beyond knowledge, no testimony can be borne, and in the giving of testimony, no facts are to be withheld.

Father, You have made me in Your image and any departure from that image demeans me. Just as a train is made for the tracks, so I am designed to run on truth. Help me to stay on track – this day and every day. In Jesus' name. Amen.

The truth about lying

FOR READING & MEDITATION – PSALM 141:1–10

'Set a guard over my mouth, O LORD; keep watch over the door of my lips.' (v3)

The truth underlying the ninth Commandment is one that as Christians we need to be so familiar with that it becomes part of the fabric of our beings. God wants us to relate to others in the way that He relates to us – in sincerity and in truth – and any departure from this is a break in the divine will and purpose. No man or woman must be helped or harmed by statements made concerning them, which are not in accordance with the facts as far as they are known.

One Bible teacher says: 'One of the greatest tests of character is this: when under pressure will this person tell a lie?' What is your attitude to a lie? It's surprising how many Christians wriggle on this hook. Some say, 'Well, there's nothing wrong with a "little" lie if it saves me from embarrassment.' Others, say, 'There is nothing wrong with lying to save someone's life.' Be careful about these rationalisations – your attitude to a lie will reveal the kind of person you are. I was an inveterate liar before I became a Christian, but divine grace cleaned me up and set me on the road of truth. It took a while for grace to overcome the old patterns, but after a while truth came out because truth had got in.

FURTHER STUDY

Col. 3:1–10;
Psa. 63:11;
Prov. 12:22;
19:5

1. What was Paul's admonition to the Colossians?

2. Who does the Lord delight in?

It has often been said that if you tell a lie you become a lie. The deepest damage of a lie is to be the one who tells the lie – the liar. He or she has to live with a person they cannot trust. That is an uneasy and divided restless place. In the Christian life there are to be no 'white lies' for they leave a black mark on the soul. This is just not the way God designed us to live.

Father, drive the truth deeply into my spirit if I should tell a lie, I become a lie. Then I have to live with a person I cannot trust. Keep my tongue from anything that would hurt You or hurt others. In Jesus' name I ask it. Amen.

FOR READING & MEDITATION – ZECHARIAH 8:1–17

'Speak the truth to each other, and render true and sound judgment in your courts' (v16)

The most straightforward application of the ninth Commandment – 'You shall not give false testimony against your neighbour' – is, of course, to evidence in a court of justice. This is why perjury is, rightly, a punishable offence, otherwise many crimes might go unpunished and the innocent will suffer.

The ninth Commandment, however, has a broader application, and it is this wider perspective that I want to focus on now. It has been said that there are seven ways in which this Commandment can be broken. The first is by libel and slander – lies that are written or spoken about someone and passed on with a malicious intention. It is hard to think of a worse form of bearing false witness than this.

A second form of bearing false witness is by talebearing. This is when someone repeats a story about someone else when there is no necessity to do so. It's deeply saddening (and damaging) that Christians who would never dream of committing murder, adultery or theft engage in this deadly sin of gossip.

A third form of bearing false witness is through the giving of a false impression. A slight has been cast upon many a person's reputation by such questions as, 'Have you heard about so and so?' 'No,' says the other person. 'Ah well, the least said the better.' Though the first speaker may be drawn no further, an unfavourable impression has been created and the innuendo has had all the deceiving effect of false witness. These kinds of statements and unfinished sentences can cause untold unhurt and divisiveness in relationships, which is why God says to speak truth and love and you'll be considered trustworthy.

FURTHER STUDY

Titus 3:1–8;
Eph. 4:31;
James 4:11

1. What was Titus to remind the people?

2. What are we doing when we slander our brother?

God, help us repent of all the things that go on in the midst of the Church which dishonour Your name. I repent of any complicity that I may have in this. Help me to be a true and honest person. For Your own dear name's sake. Amen.

No meaner form of rebellion

FOR READING & MEDITATION – PROVERBS 13:1–9

'The righteous hate what is false' (v5)

We continue looking at the remaining four of the seven ways in which we can bear false witness. The fourth way at first may seem surprising, but we can break the ninth Commandment to not bear false testimony against our neighbour simply by our silence. If we hear someone being misrepresented and we know the words being said are not true, then if we keep silent, we are as guilty of false witness as the person who utters the disparagement.

A fifth way is by imputing to a person a wrong motive. 'Have you heard how well so-and-so is doing in business?' 'Ah, but how do you think he's got where he has? Don't you think he must have been involved in some shady business practices?' I have no hesitation in saying that to impute to another an ulterior, selfish or ignoble motive is to bear false witness against that person. A sixth way is flattery. To tell people things you do not believe to be true simply to please them, or to pander to their vanity, or win them over to your side in some issue. Manipulation is always ugly and never pleasing to God.

FURTHER STUDY

1 Tim. 4:1–12;
Prov. 22:11;
2 Cor. 8:7;
Eph. 4:15

1. What was Timothy to set an example in?

2. What are we to do in love?

The seventh way the ninth Commandment can be broken is by an untrue testimonial. Whenever we give unwarranted praise, provide a testimonial to character that is untrue, or recommend an unsuitable person simply because he or she is our friend, we inflict injury upon the one requesting the testimonial.

Can you see now how subtle a danger false witness is? There is no lower form of rebellion against God and one's fellow human beings than that of creating impressions in the minds of others that are simply not true.

Father, help me to see that the reason why You are straight with me is because You love me too much to let me live with things that lessen my character. Save me from telling a lie, spreading a lie, or living a lie. In Jesus' name I pray. Amen.

Desiring and coveting

FOR READING & MEDITATION – ROMANS 13:1–14

'The commandments... "Do not covet,"... are summed up in this one rule: "Love your neighbour as yourself."' (v9)

The last and tenth Word of the Decalogue is in one way radically different from those that have preceded it: 'You shall not covet your neighbour's house... his manservant or maidservant, his ox or donkey, or anything that belongs to your neighbour' (Exod. 20:17). All the preceding Commandments have forbidden overt acts; this one cuts right through to inner attitudes. This is an issue of contentment and thankfulness and it links to the earlier Commandment of developing trust in God for His provision. Breaking any of the other nine Commandments will sooner or later be spotted by others, but the tenth Commandment may be broken without another person being aware of it. The issue it deals with is that of covetousness. But what is covetousness? The word 'covet' means 'to strongly desire something that belongs to someone else'. This can become a dangerous downward path. Let me unpack this a little more. When we covet something that God has not provided, it can, in turn, lead to resentment of God. Does that mean that when I see a friend with a model of car that I myself would like to possess, I am guilty of coveting? No. What about when I see a painting on the wall of a neighbour's house and I want to get one like it? Is that coveting? No.

Covetousness occurs when the object desired is out of reach and it continues to burn in my heart demanding some kind of action. This is greed at its worst. The whole force of the Commandment lies in the words: your neighbour's. I repeat, it is not wrong to desire a wife, a manservant or maidservant, or an ox – it becomes wrong if one desires to take it from someone else.

FURTHER STUDY

Jer. 6:1–13;
Ezek. 33:30–31;
Phil. 3:10–14

1. What was said of the priests and prophets?

2. What were the children of Israel doing to Ezekiel?

Father, let the truth sink deep within me that Your warnings associated with greed are the signs of Your love. Help me to work with that love – not against it. In Jesus' name. Amen.

'Much wants more'

FOR READING & MEDITATION – LUKE 12:13–21

'Be on your guard against all kinds of greed; a man's life does not consist in the abundance of his possessions.' (v15)

We touched yesterday on the fact that there is a great difference between desiring something and coveting it. Without desire, human life would no doubt be impoverished. Our desire for social approval makes us wash our face and comb our hair. Our desire for respect leads us to be careful about the things we do and the way we behave.

Buddha taught that desire itself was the source of evil in the world and he claimed that if we eliminated all desire we would eliminate all evil – Nirvana. But I don't believe it is desire that is wrong – it is inordinate desire, the desiring of that which is unlawful. As we said yesterday, it is not wrong to desire a house, a wife, a servant, a painting, a car, but it is wrong to continue to be driven by the things our neighbour possesses when there is just no way we can legitimately have those things for ourselves. Desire passes into covetousness when it runs rampant over our own reason and the rights of others. You see, when desire passes into covetousness it then has within it the potential to kill, steal, or lie in order to get what it wants. It is the attitude that says: 'I want what I want and I don't care what I have to do to get it.'

FURTHER STUDY

2 Sam. 11;
1 Kings 21:1–16

1. What did David's covetousness lead to?

2. What did Ahab's covetousness lead to?

One of Aesop's fables tells of a man who killed a goose that laid golden eggs. The story concludes with this moral: 'Much wants more and loses all.' That is the consequence of covetousness – it stops at nothing to get what it wants and breaks so many laws of conscience on the way to getting it that it finishes up by not wanting what it gets. When we can learn to trust in God for His provision we arrive at a place of contentment, and contentment overcomes covetousness.

Father, I am so thankful that you have not just saved us but help us to live life well. May I learn this day to be truly content in You and all You provide. In Jesus' name. Amen.

Next Issue

NOV/DEC 2018

Strong at the Broken Places

In our fallen world, all of us will know brokenness of some kind. Things happen – often beyond our control – that can leave us feeling crushed or overwhelmed. But we have a sure and certain hope in the assurance that God's power is made perfect in weakness (2 Cor. 12:9), and that He can transform *any* situation for good.

Next issue, discover how God can use the things that break us to build us up, and how we can, in the words of Ernest Hemingway, be 'strong at the broken places'.

Every Day
with Jesus

NOV/DEC 2018

Strong at the
Broken Places

'My grace is sufficient for you, for my power is made perfect in weakness.'
2 Corinthians 12:9

Living life with Jesus. Every day   CWR

Also available as eBook/
eSubscription

Obtain your copy from CWR, a Christian bookshop or your National Distributor.
If you would like to take out a subscription, see the order form at the back of these notes.

The reason for the law

FOR READING & MEDITATION – ROMANS 7:7–13

'Indeed I would not have known what sin was except through the law.'
(v7)

We continue examining the nature of covetousness, which we have seen can best be described as the desire for what cannot lawfully be possessed – the desiring of things that circumstances have put out of reach. Desiring is not wrong, but when desire is directed to a wrong end, it can soon turn into covetousness.

The instruction covering covetousness identifies the presence of greed in our hearts in a way that is sharp and powerful. We have already noted that when we covet something that God has not provided it can, in turn, lead to resentment of God. Equally, when we desire something more than our relationship with God, it can soon become an idol.

FURTHER STUDY

Gal. 3;
Rom. 3:20;
1 Tim. 1:9

1. Why were the Galatians foolish?

2. What is the purpose of the law?

This is the point Paul is making in today's passage when, in his great argument on the relationship of the law to sin, he says: 'I would not have known what sin was except through the law. For I would not have known what coveting really was if the law had not said, "Do not covet."' Paul is highlighting for us that sin is so deeply hidden within the recesses of our being that we would not be able to recognise it if God's law did not reveal it. Sin is present in every life, revealed by the desire to possess unreachable things, and this is only really unearthed when God says, 'You shall not covet.'

People sometimes say about this Commandment: 'But it is impossible to prevent covetousness becoming desire.' This very statement emphasises the condition of humanity and shows why the law was given. Well will it be when we allow God to search our spirit that we might be drawn to Him who alone is able to deal with the darkest recesses of our nature.

Father, I am thankful for the law and I am thankful for grace. Both were needed to bring me to Yourself. The law showed me how badly I needed saving and grace reached down and saved me. All praise and glory be to Your precious name. Amen.

No other God

FOR READING & MEDITATION – EPHESIANS 5:1–21

*'But among you there must not be even a hint of sexual immorality,
or of any kind of impurity, or of greed' (v3)*

Today we ask ourselves: was the command prohibiting covetousness kept to the last because it was the least of all the Commandments? I do not believe so. It is, in fact, probably the most far-reaching and comprehensive of them all. Covetousness affects every part of our lives. It makes people greedy and acquisitive and causes them to steal. It drives people to ignore the needs of others and trample on their rights; in some cases covetousness will even kill in order to get what it wants. It gives rise to the unbridled lust that pushes people into adultery and betrayal, and it breaks down trust between individuals, causing people to lie about themselves and each other.

Covetousness destroys the bloom and beauty of those characteristics which Paul calls the 'fruit of the Spirit', turning love to hate, joy to sorrow, peace to heartache, longsuffering to impatience, kindness to cruelty, generosity to miserliness, faithfulness to infidelity, meekness to arrogance and self-control to indiscipline and self-indulgence. A damaged spirit that makes false witness possible is motivated by a covetous aspiration far more often than is perhaps apparent at first.

The last of God's Ten Words, covetousness, proves not only that the soul is out of sync with God, but also that it is dissatisfied with Him. Covetousness says: 'I can't trust God to give me what I need, therefore I shall reach out and obtain it myself.' His first Word and the last Word are very closely linked and all those between are conditioned by them. If a person has no other God but Jehovah Elohim, the God who is there, then they will desire nothing other than that which God supplies.

FURTHER STUDY

1 Tim. 6:1–10;
Prov. 15:27;
Eccl. 5:10;
Phil. 4:11–12

1. What did Paul say was great gain?

2. What was Paul's testimony?

Father, perhaps the reason why I get so taken up with other things is because I am not taken up with You. May my desire for You be so strong and powerful that it will keep all other desires under control. In Jesus' name I pray. Amen.

The rare jewel

FOR READING & MEDITATION – ROMANS 5:12–21

'But where sin increased, grace increased all the more.' (v20)

The last Word of the Decalogue: 'You shall not covet,' brings every man and woman who honestly faces it to the place of dependency. It may be that as we have examined the nine other Commandments we have a measure of intactness and integrity still left, but in the light of this last searching Word, who can claim to be guiltless?

It was Paul who, after many years of Christian experience, could say, when reviewing his old life as a Hebrew of the Hebrews, 'in regard to the law, a Pharisee... as for legalistic righteousness, faultless' (Phil. 3:5–6). Yet when he faced this last Commandment, 'You shall not covet,' Paul had to say that he found the Word brought not satisfaction but dissatisfaction. There are perhaps many reading these lines who can look at some of the Ten Commandments – Commandments like, 'You shall not murder' – and say, 'I am not guilty,' but is there anyone anywhere in the whole world who can say they have never coveted what someone else has instead of trusting in God. And covetousness does not just stop at possessions; it can include the gifts or position another has too.

FURTHER STUDY

2 Cor. 12:1–12;
2 Tim. 2:1;
Phil. 4:19

1. What was Paul able to boast?

2. What was Paul's admonition to Timothy?

Jesus is the only one who can take us from covetousness to contentment, and He does it by helping us learn to trust in Him. When the apostle Paul was under house arrest in Rome, chained to a Roman soldier, he shared how he had learned, as the Puritan writer Jeremiah Burroughs put it, the secret of that rare jewel of Christian contentment: 'I have learned the secret of being content in any and every situation, whether well fed or hungry, whether living in plenty or in want'. How did he do this?: 'I can do everything through him who gives me strength' (Phil. 4:13).

God, these words echo how I feel. You have given me a clear understanding of Your law and for that I am grateful – now give me more grace. In Jesus' name I ask it. Amen.

Delight, not duty

FOR READING & MEDITATION – HEBREWS 8:1–13

*'I will put my laws in their minds and write them on their hearts.
I will be their God, and they will be my people.' (v10)*

Although we may have completed our exploration of God's Ten Words, our meditation on the subject has not yet been concluded. There are some other issues that now need to be brought into perspective, and over the few final days we have left I want to explore these with you.

The first is this: what is the role of the Ten Commandments in the life of the Christian? If we say we are saved by grace, through faith, how does the law fit into the picture? As we saw at the beginning of our studies, there are many Christians in today's Church who claim that once we are saved we are no longer under the judgment of the law of God and therefore the Ten Commandments have no meaning for a true believer. In my view this 'lawless' version of Christianity is a travesty of the truth – a scandalous misinterpretation of what the Bible is saying. Although it is true that we can never be saved by the law – for the simple reason that no one in their own strength can keep it – this does not mean that the law no longer applies.

FURTHER STUDY

2 Cor. 3:1–15;
Psa. 37:23–31;
Heb. 10:15–16

1. What did Paul say of the Corinthians?

2. What is the result of having God's law in our hearts?

The passage before us today sums up what other books of the New Testament teach us (for example, Rom. 5:5; Gal. 4:6–7) – that when we come to faith, the Holy Spirit writes God's law on our hearts and helps us to live by them. And He not only helps us to live by them, He helps us to do it lovingly and joyously. This is the new way of living that the New Testament holds out for us. It introduces us to the new and exciting truth that once the Holy Spirit abides within our hearts, following the law is no longer a daily duty but a daily delight. As the psalmist said: 'for I delight in your commands because I love them' (Psa. 119:47).

My Father and my God, I see that when I became a Christian, I not only came into a new world but a new world came into me. Now I see the law in a different light – Your light. What a difference this makes! Father, I am so thankful. Amen.

Fences along the road of grace

FOR READING & MEDITATION – TITUS 2:1–15

'For the grace of God... teaches us to say "No" to ungodliness'
(vv11–12)

We continue to explore further the erroneous belief that once we become Christians we are free from any responsibility to obey the Ten Commandments. Before going any further, let me clarify my use of the word 'law'. By 'law' I mean the Ten Commandments. There were other laws in Israel – the ceremonial law, for example – that do not apply to us who live in New Testament times, for they were abrogated by the death of Jesus. But the issues raised in the Ten Commandments still hold true for today.

FURTHER STUDY

Rom. 7–8;
Matt. 5:17–20

1. What conflict did Paul experience?

2. Why did Jesus say He had come?

Let us focus on the text that is often repeated by those who advocate that once we are saved by grace the law no longer applies: 'For sin shall not be your master, because you are not under law, but under grace' (Rom. 6:14). What Paul is saying in the whole of the epistle to the Romans is that no Christian need depend on the keeping of the Ten Commandments as the means of his or her salvation. Paul does not mean that the law of God is abolished, but that the Christian does not look to the law for either justification or sanctification.

Forgive me for repeating the point I made yesterday, but I feel it is necessary. Once the Holy Spirit comes into our hearts, instead of resisting the law, we can rejoice in it. And why? Because we sense within us a new strength that enables us to do the things God asks of us. The road of grace, which has been opened up to us through the death of Christ, has not been fenced by a long list of legalistic rules but by God's loving design in His moral law, the Ten Commandments. We may be under a new law of love, but Scripture clearly teaches that love is the fulfilling, the completeness, of the law.

Father, help me to get this, for I see it is a deeply important issue. Show me even more clearly that being under grace does not mean I no longer need to keep Your law, but that grace is there to help me keep it. In Jesus' name. Amen.

Law or grace?

FOR READING & MEDITATION – MATTHEW 23:15–28

'You blind men! Which is greater: the gift, or the altar that makes the gift sacred?' (v19)

Having now dealt with the error that once we become Christians we are no longer required to obey the Commandments of God, we look at another problem that arises in connection with this issue – the Christian who is saved but comes to depend for his or her salvation more on the keeping of the law than on divine grace. This is often labelled 'legalism'. The sad thing about those who are caught up in this is that they have hardly any awareness of the fact that they are working to be saved, rather than working because they are saved.

The Pharisees of Jesus' day were a good example of legalism. They took the Ten Commandments and added a lot more of their own, so that by the time Jesus came they had a list of 365 don'ts – one for every day of the year! And they meticulously observed all their rules. Legalists are not content unless they are surrounded by rules, because they feel safe (or saved) only when they are keeping to them. And most legalists I have known add to the Ten Commandments every cultural and traditional taboo they can lay their hands on. Since they are resting on their performance for their salvation rather than on the grace that God provides, the more rules they have to keep, the better they like it.

FURTHER STUDY

Gal. 4:1–11;
Isa. 29:13;
Matt. 23:23

1. What was Paul's concern for the Galatians?

2. What was our Lord's complaint against the Pharisees?

You can be sure that a legalist has a lot more don'ts than dos, and this kind of living makes life a daily grind and but a poor reflection of what God desires for His children. How often the Lord Jesus had to expose the legalistic rules of the Pharisees in order to teach the true meaning of God's law. If God gave me one wish, it would be to blast legalism right out of the Church.

Father, help me come to grips with this issue, for I see I can be snared without realising it. Help me get it straight that my dependence is on You and not on keeping the rules. I ask this in Jesus' all-powerful and saving name. Amen.

Love and grace

FOR READING & MEDITATION – 1 CORINTHIANS 8:1–13

'if what I eat causes my brother to fall into sin, I will never eat meat again, so that I will not cause him to fall.' (v13)

We continue with our meditation on legalism. As we saw, sadly, legalists don't feel safe unless they have around them as many rules as possible. They thrive on rules – but not in the way that produces life and spiritual growth. And many of the rules they wrap around themselves are cultural and traditional rather than scriptural.

A letter written in the second century giving advice on how to live the Christian life reads: 'Don't wear coloured clothes; get rid of everything in your house that is not white. Stop sleeping on soft pillows. Sell your musical instruments and don't take any more warm baths.' Legalism takes relative matters and turns them into absolutes; it comes up with human ideas and claims that these have to be kept if a person is to be saved.

FURTHER STUDY

Col. 2:13–23;
Heb. 7:18; 8:13

1. What has God cancelled?

2. What were the Colossians still doing?

There is a way of dealing with matters that are non-absolutes – it is by nurturing a sensitive conscience. Paul talks about it in today's passage. In one situation he would eat meat offered to idols, but in another situation he would not. Contradictory behaviour? No, he had developed a conscience that understood the difference between what was relative and what was absolute. And it is this – a mature conscience – that prevents us from falling into the trap of legalism. Let us remember that these Ten Words were given to help and guide us to live in a rich relationship with God and others, and importantly God didn't reveal these great truths until after the children of Israel's deliverance from slavery. Knowing the condition of the human heart He knew our propensity to be more comfortable with self-dependency for our salvation than God-dependency and grace. Let's not forget we have been redeemed by God's great love and grace. And that's amazing!

Father, I have prayed before for a clean conscience – now I pray for one that is neither under-sensitive nor over-sensitive, but is mature and balanced and always open to Your Spirit. In Christ's name I ask it. Amen.

A new commandment

FOR READING & MEDITATION – JOHN 13:21–38

*'A new command I give you: Love one another. As I have loved you,
so you must love one another.' (v34)*

The text for today highlights for us an extremely important issue – the relationship of law to love. The law and love are not incompatible or mutually exclusive but are inter-related and inter-dependent: love needs law to guide it. In his book *Christ the Controversialist*, John Stott wrote: 'What the New Testament says about law and love is not, "If you love you can break the law," but rather, "If you love you will keep the law."'

Jesus is the embodiment of love, but on one occasion He said: 'Do not think that I have come to abolish the Law or the Prophets... but to fulfil them' (Matt. 5:17). In His life and teaching He fulfilled the law – both in word, deed and intention. However, just before leaving the world He announced to His disciples a new commandment that has been described as the badge of true discipleship – a command to love. This new commandment revealed the purpose behind His coming. It was not to set aside the law but that the requirements of the law might be met through the obedience that springs not from duty but from love. To break any one of these Ten Commandments is a breach of love. It follows, therefore, that if love directs and controls the life, then there can be no such breach.

FURTHER STUDY

John 14:15–31;
1 John 2:17;
John 15:10

1. How is our love for Christ expressed?

2. How did Jesus demonstrate this?

This is true both of a person's relationship with God and of our relationship with others. Listen to how Paul puts it when talking about our relationship with others: 'Let no debt remain outstanding, except the continuing debt to love one another, for he who loves his fellow-man has fulfilled the law' (Rom. 13:8). To love perfectly is to fulfil perfectly the law which was spoken in love. And where there is no love there can be no real understanding of the law.

Lord Jesus, my heart is bowed in deepest gratitude at the wonder of Your amazing love. Your love has loved me into loving – loving You, loving others and loving myself. I am eternally grateful. Thank You, my Saviour. Amen.

So simple yet magnificent

FOR READING & MEDITATION – ROMANS 13:8–14

'Therefore love is the fulfilment of the law.' (v10)

We saw yesterday that every breach of these Ten Words is a breach of love, and when love directs life there is no such breach. So important is this simple but magnificent principle that we spend our last day together applying it to each of the Ten Commandments. If we love God absolutely, then we will not be able to find room for another god and the first of the Ten Words is fulfilled. Supreme love for God also means that we will not suffer anything to stand between us and Him, and so all idols are broken to pieces. Out of love will spring a reverence of His name and a life worthy of the one who lends His name to us. Love understands the principle behind the Sabbath and will not just cease from work, but will also gladly engage with rest and remembrance.

FURTHER STUDY

1 Cor. 13;
Jude 21;
2 Thess. 3:5

1. What was Paul's desire for the Thessalonians?

2. How are the characteristics of love in 1 Corinthians also seen in the Ten Commandments?

In the second part of the Commandments, love for God means we will honour our parents and quench all thoughts of hatred towards others. Love treats another's property with respect and keeps our thoughts and conduct towards the opposite sex pure. When love is the filter of what we speak, it arrests the faintest whisper of false witness against others. And love for God gives us a contentment with ourselves and what we have that leaves no room in the heart for coveting anything but Him and the greatest thing – love (1 Cor. 13:13). When men and women learn to love, then Sinai, the mountain of fire, holds no fear. They can stand tall against it, knowing that as Jesus lives and loves in them, thoughts will be born, words will be spoken and deeds will be done – in love. Then in thought and word and deed, the law will be fulfilled.

Father, from this hour forward let the simple but magnificent principle of love flood my life and fill my days. In Jesus' name I pray. Amen.

Order form

4 Easy Ways To Order

1. Phone in your credit card order: **01252 784700** (Mon–Fri, 9.30am – 4.30pm)
2. Visit our online store at **www.cwr.org.uk/shop**
3. Send this form together with your payment to: **CWR, Waverley Abbey House, Waverley Lane, Farnham, Surrey GU9 8EP**
4. Visit a Christian bookshop

For a list of our National Distributors, who supply countries outside the UK, visit www.cwr.org.uk/distributors

Your Details (required for orders and donations)

Full Name:	CWR ID No. (if known):
Home Address:	
	Postcode:
Telephone No. (for queries):	Email:

Due to forthcoming changes in the law, we need you to confirm that you wish to receive information from CWR by ticking the relevant boxes: **I want to be kept informed of CWR's ministry by email ☐ by post ☐**

Publications

TITLE	QTY	PRICE	TOTAL
		Total Publications	
UK P&P: up to £24.99 = **£2.99**; £25.00 and over = **FREE**			
Elsewhere P&P: up to £10 = **£4.95**; £10.01 – £50 = **£6.95**; £50.01 – £99.99 = **£10**; £100 and over = **£30**			
Total Publications and P&P (please allow 14 days for delivery)		**A**	

Ⓔ ✉ All CWR adult Bible reading notes are also available in **eBook** and **email subscription** format. Visit **www.cwr.org.uk** for further information.

Subscriptions* (non direct debit)

	QTY	PRICE (including P&P)			TOTAL
		UK	Europe	Elsewhere	
Every Day with Jesus (1yr, 6 issues)		£16.95	£20.95		
Large Print *Every Day with Jesus* (1yr, 6 issues)		£16.95	£20.95	Please contact	
Inspiring Women Every Day (1yr, 6 issues)		£16.95	£20.95	nearest	
Life Every Day (Jeff Lucas) (1yr, 6 issues)		£16.95	£20.95	National	
Mettle: 15–18s (1yr, 3 issues)		£14.75	£17.60	Distributor	
YP's: 11–14s (1yr, 6 issues)		£16.95	£20.95	or CWR direct	
Topz: 7–11s (1yr, 6 issues)		£16.95	£20.95		
Total Subscriptions (subscription prices already include postage and packing)				**B**	

*Only use this section for subscriptions paid for by credit/debit card or cheque. For Direct Debit subscriptions see overleaf.

Please circle which issue you would like your subscription to commence from:

JAN/FEB MAR/APR MAY/JUN JUL/AUG SEP/OCT NOV/DEC

Mettle **JAN–APR MAY–AUG SEP–DEC**

Continued overleaf >>

Payment Details

☐ I enclose a cheque/PO made payable to CWR for the amount of: **£** _____

☐ Please charge my credit/debit card.

Cardholder's Name (in BLOCK CAPITALS) _____

Card No. ☐☐☐☐ ☐☐☐☐ ☐☐☐☐ ☐☐☐☐

Expires End ☐☐ ☐☐   Security Code ☐☐☐

Gift to CWR ☐ Please send me an acknowledgement of my gift   **C** ☐

Gift Aid (your home address required, see overleaf)

giftaid it I am a UK taxpayer and want CWR to reclaim the tax on all my donations for the four years prior to this year **and on** all donations I make from the date of this Gift Aid declaration until further notice.*

Taxpayer's Full Name (in BLOCK CAPITALS) _____

Signature _____ **Date** _____

*I am a UK taxpayer and understand that if I pay less Income Tax and/or Capital Gains Tax than the amount of Gift Aid claimed on all my donations in that tax year it is my responsibility to pay any difference.

GRAND TOTAL (Total of A, B & C) ☐

Subscriptions by Direct Debit (UK bank account holders only)

One-year subscriptions cost £16.95 (except *Mettle*: £14.75) and include UK delivery. Please tick relevant boxes and fill in the form below.

		Issue to commence from		
☐ *Every Day with Jesus* (1yr, 6 issues)	☐ *Mettle*: 15–18s (1yr, 3 issues)	☐ Jan/Feb ☐ Jul/Aug	*Mettle*	☐ Jan–Apr
☐ Large Print *Every Day with Jesus* (1yr, 6 issues)	☐ *YP's*: 11–14s (1yr, 6 issues)	☐ Mar/Apr ☐ Sep/Oct		☐ May–Aug
☐ *Inspiring Women Every Day* (1yr, 6 issues)	☐ *Topz*: 7–11s (1yr, 6 issues)	☐ May/Jun ☐ Nov/Dec		☐ Sep–Dec
☐ *Life Every Day* (Jeff Lucas) (1yr, 6 issues)				

CWR Instruction to your Bank or Building Society to pay by Direct Debit

DIRECT Debit

Please fill in the form and send to: CWR, Waverley Abbey House,
Waverley Lane, Farnham, Surrey GU9 8EP
Name and full postal address of your Bank or Building Society

To: The Manager   Bank/Building Society

Address _____

_____

Postcode _____

Name(s) of Account Holder(s)

_____

Branch Sort Code

☐☐ ☐☐ ☐☐

Bank/Building Society Account Number

☐☐☐☐☐☐☐☐

Originator's Identification Number

4	2	0	4	8	7

Reference

☐☐☐☐☐☐☐☐☐☐☐☐☐☐☐☐☐

Instruction to your Bank or Building Society

Please pay CWR Direct Debits from the account detailed in this Instruction subject to the safeguards assured by the Direct Debit Guarantee.
I understand that this Instruction may remain with CWR and, if so, details will be passed electronically to my Bank/Building Society.

Signature(s)

_____

Date

_____

Banks and Building Societies may not accept Direct Debit Instructions for some types of account